G. GRUBB,

Corn Factor, Seedsman,

Hay & Straw Dealer.

Agent for Carter's "Tested" Seeds, Spratt's Patent Specialities, Clarke's Melox, Puppy Cakes, etc.,

Victoria Dog Biscuits, Osoko, etc.

Coton Road, Nuneaton.

Man

G.   High-grade

Elliot Cycles,

Fitted with Palmer, Continental, Dunlop or Clipper Tyres.

MOTORCYCLE (adjustable Pulley and Switches).
See our RACING CYCLE (1910 Model).

Enamelling and Plating done on the Premises.
Cycle and Motor Repairs of all kinds at lowest prices
by Experienced Workmen.
Agent for Bradbury's Motor Cycles & Sewing
Machines.

ESTABLISHED 1855.

John Wilkinson & Son,

11 & 12, Abbey St., Nuneaton.

Removal in Own Vans by
Road or Rail.

TELEPHONE No. 5x1.

Removals to any distance.
Estimates Free.

Telephone No. 5x1.

COMPLETE HOUSE FURNISHERS

JOHN WILKINSON & SON

COMPLETE HOUSE FURNISHERS AND CARPET WAREHOUSEMEN.

If you desire to Furnish in a comfortable, artistic, and durable manner, with due regard to economy, you can best do so by making your purchases at the above address

Every attention is given to customers and there is a large and varied Stock of up-to-date Goods to select from.

MODERATE PRICES.

Removals undertaken to all parts.   Only careful and competent men employed.

Practical Upholstery in all its Branches.   Outside Sun Blinds and Blinds of every kind made and repaired.

PATTERNS AND ESTIMATES FREE

Delicious Roast Pork,
Ham, Tongue, - -
Beef, Home-made
Pork Pies, - -
Polonies, -
Sausages, and
Potted
Meats.

Fresh
Daily

Birch's Restaurant.

Hot Dinners Daily.

COOK

and Purveyor of

MEATS,

Queen's Road,
NUNEATON.

PARTIES CATERED FOR.

Established over 50 Years.

WILLIAM GREEN,

DEALER IN

Antique and Modern Furniture,

45, UPPER ABBEY ST., NUNEATON.

Buy at the Cheapest Market.

You may fool all the People some of the time, or some of the People all the time. There is a lot of truth and wisdom in those few words. If you call at the above address you will not be fooled at any time.

I GIVE VALUE FOR MONEY.

C000298999

NUNEATON
A History

The Co-operative Society procession on its 21st Anniversary Treats, 1905, turns out of Attleborough Road into Bull Street.

NUNEATON
A History

E.A. Veasey

Phillimore

2002

Published by
PHILLIMORE & CO. LTD
Shopwyke Manor Barn, Chichester, West Sussex

© E.A. Veasey, 2002

ISBN 1 86077 215 3

Printed and bound in Great Britain by
BIDDLES LTD
Guildford, Surrey

Contents

List of Illustrations

Frontispiece: Attleborough: Co-operative Society procession, 1905

Acknowledgements

I offer my sincere thanks to the staffs of Warwick, Stratford Birthplace Trust and Lichfield Record Offices for their help and guidance over many years of research. Also to Nuneaton Library, especially successive local history librarians who have willingly made available the huge repository of information which they have collected. More personally I am ever grateful to the late Arthur Gooder and his widow Eileen who first introduced me to local history research and tried to instil a rigorous and scholarly approach to the past. I also owe a great debt to the local history research group students whose work over some thirty years has contributed much to this book. Lastly, I must thank two family members: Simon for rescuing the text from frequent computer crises, and my wife Pat for her support over the years of study.

The illustrations are mainly taken from my own photographs, with copies of others and postcards, most of which are out of copyright or the owners untraceable. The following have most generously provided photographs: Jennifer Burton, 142; John Burton, 4, 22, 29, 53, 79, 116, 117, 118, 121, 147; May Dawkins, 11; the late T.W. Evans, 91; Mr T. Hackney, 13; Margaret Lawrence, 48; the late Fred Phillips, 46, 64; *Heartland Evening News*, 8, 32, 35, 43, 139, 140.

Foreword

For me, local history is the story of a place and its people through time. It is continuity of growth and development, setbacks and decay. The abiding question is, how did the place get to where it is at the present time?

Because there is no known continuity I have omitted the earliest peoples who lived on the heights at Corley and Oldbury and left their stone implements scattered over the area. I have also left out the Romano-British with their settlement at Mancetter and kiln sites across the borough. Neither is this the story of great people (apart from Chapter Seven) or of great national events. It is the history of quite ordinary Nuneaton people, the economic forces which shaped their lives, and the social conditions in which they lived. Our past is their present.

To walk in Nuneaton is to walk through its history. This the illustrations with their captions attempt to do. In them the informed eye sees evidence of the changing town and its people's lives; the insignificant becomes important when placed in context.

For Emily, Tomas, Jessica and Georgina,
the youngest generation,
to whom I am largely history!

One

Ea-tun and its Neighbours
from Settlement to Domesday

The history of the Nuneaton area as a group of continuous settlements starts with the coming of the Anglo-Saxons. When they came or by what route is not recorded. The one shred of positive local evidence is a pagan Anglo-Saxon drinking vessel, excavated in Furnace Fields, Bedworth, in 1939, which has been dated to the fifth or sixth century. Thus it seems likely that the earliest settlers had reached this area by A.D. 600 at the latest. Because of its central position, the Nuneaton area could have been colonised by any one of three major invasion routes. One group of settlers penetrated the Midlands by way of the Wash and the Welland Valley, probably reaching south Leicestershire. A second group came via the Thames and Avon towards Coventry and Rugby. The third route is the most likely for Nuneaton, coming from the Humber, Trent and Tame to Tamworth and, finally, following the course of the Anker upstream into this area.

The early settlers did, however, leave one permanent record. They named almost every place in the area. Only two names—Anker and the 'man' element in Mancetter—are possibly Celtic; the rest are composed of Anglo-Saxon, and occasionally Viking, words. Domesday Book lists most of the names which were in existence in 1086 and presumably there before the Normans came. Place-name scholars have reconstructed the Anglo-Saxon words which lie beneath the Norman versions. The names

describe what was actually here during the six hundred years of the pre-Conquest period, allowing us a glimpse at the remote, hidden origins of the area. Each name has two parts: the first is either descriptive or a personal name; the second is one of five common elements: *tun, ingtun, worth, cote* or *leah*. The closest meaning for *tun* is tribal farm; the holding of a large family with retainers and slaves. *Ingtun* and *worth* also mean farm, the latter being enclosed with a bank and ditch. *Cote* means cottage and *leah* a clearing taken out of the surrounding forest.

Ea-tun the farm by water, Ceolfrid's Cottage (Chilvers Coton) and Whaet's Farm (Weddington) reveal how sparse the settlement was and how isolated these places were. They are not towns nor even villages. They were small scattered habitations with their associated farmlands gradually being cut out of the forest and connected by trackways, the origin of many of our modern roads.

Attleborough and Stockingford do not appear in Domesday Book because they were part of Earl Aubrey's manor of Ea-tun. The earliest recorded mention of Attleborough comes in A.D. 1150 as *Atreberga*. The elements are *Aetla* and *beorge* meaning Aetla's hill. This seems to pose a problem since most of Attleborough is flat and low-lying. Recent research suggests that *beorge* means barrow (tumulus) or earthwork, as in Burrow Hill, Corley. Thus 'Aetla's beorge' might describe a long-lost prehistoric tumulus in the

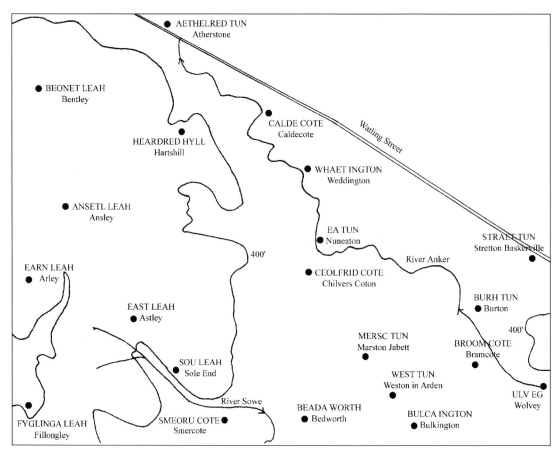

1   The Anglo-Saxon settlement. This map shows all the Domesday manors in the Nuneaton area. Their existence in 1086 implies an Anglo-Saxon origin. Most of the sites are along the Anker and Sowe valleys. Settlements above the 400-foot contour line are fewer and probably later.

Attleborough area. Stockingford first appears in 1157 as *Stoccingford*. It derives from Old English *stocc*, to root up trees. Stockingford, then has its origin in a man-made forest clearing by a ford across a stream—probably the one which still runs through Whittleford.

When mapped, the place-names show a possible pattern of settlement. Of the 21 local Domesday names, 16 are sited below the 400-foot contour line and only five above it. The earliest settlers, being farmers, chose to colonise the well-watered but well-drained plain lying above the Anker and Sowe rivers, and pushed their estate boundaries to local landmarks, usually streams. Later settlements were thus

restricted to the higher ground to the west. Astley, for example, is the east clearing of an earlier settlement, probably Fillongley, which must have been already in existence. Domesday Book also suggests that the settlements to the west were still relatively undeveloped. While half of Bedworth's 600 acres of open-field arable land can be deduced from Domesday Book, Smercote and Soul End, further west, had no recorded arable at all.

The origins of Ea-tun are as obscure and conjectural as the settlement of the whole area, though there are several clues which allow an informed guess about its original siting. As the name suggests, it was by the water: the River

Anker. Church Street and Bond Gate lie inside a deep river bend which would form a defensive barrier on three sides. Within the river bend stand the parish church and the town mill, whose sites could have a continuity of use back before Domesday. There is no record of a pre-Conquest church but, since the Anglo-Saxons became Christian, there must have been at least a consecrated place, with a church being built on the site at a later time. The mill was recorded in Domesday Book so it must have pre-dated the Conquest. Again, the roads to Coventry, Atherstone, Burton on Trent, Leicester and Lutterworth all converge in the same area, possibly indicating a good river crossing, a meeting place and a settlement. The best clue is topographical. East of Church Street and Bond Gate run Vicarage and Back Streets—a typical village plan—the house plots running from the village street to the back lane which gave access to the rear of the properties. These extremely long plots on both sides of the street are in marked contrast to the later, more regularly shaped, medieval burgage plots.

The original farm by the water had become over several centuries an Anglo-Saxon vill or township. How it developed is not known, though during the Viking period Watling Street marked the Midlands border between Danelaw and Saxon England and Ea-tun was a frontier town with all the attendant dangers. Griff (pit or hollow) and Keresley (Kaerer's clearing) are probably of Viking origin and may indicate incursions across the border.

Though its development is lost, the picture does emerge of the vill of Ea-tun at the time of the Conquest. From its holy site (or possible church) standing on a slight rise a village street, lined on both sides with cottages and farm houses, ran down to, and beyond, the mill. If

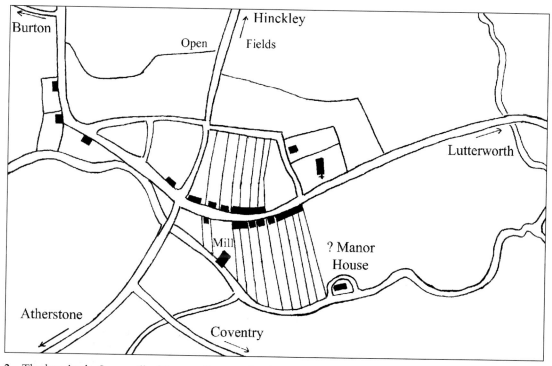

2 The late Anglo-Saxon vill of Ea-tun. Topographical evidence suggests that the village street and its back lane ran northwards across a sweeping bend of the river. Only the mill is listed in Domesday Book but a church site almost certainly existed at the south end of the street.

3   Nuneaton Mill, post-1886. The site of the Domesday mill with its dam and millponds probably remained unchanged until milling ceased in 1959. The early 19th-century red-brick mill burned down in 1885 and was replaced by the last, blue-brick, mill.

4   The Church Street/Vicarage Street area in 1926. This aerial view shows clearly how the early village layout, with its extremely long house plots, survived until the mid-20th century. Edward Melly's large house at the south end is the only major change to the original plan.

Ea-tun had a manor house, there are two possible sites. One is at the north end of the vill where there was a croft in the medieval period called Hall Close (now part of the Trent Valley Station area). Alternatively, at the south end, opposite the church, there was a field called Moat Close which shows on 19th-century maps a moated site close to the river. Beyond the back lane of the vill were several enclosed crofts and then the immense open fields stretched eastwards across the plain to Watling Street. West of the river, the land was almost certainly part of the lord's demesne and, as yet, largely uncolonised woodland, part of the ancient forest of Arden.

The earliest description of the local vills appears in Domesday Book, the survey made in 1086 for William the Conqueror to determine who held what land and how much it was worth. The Nuneaton extracts are as follows:

Nuneaton
Earl Aubrey held Etone from the king. Harding held it before 1066. Land for 26 ploughs. In lordship 3 ploughs and 3 slaves; 44 villagers, 6 freedmen and 10 smallholders with 16 ploughs. A mill at 32d; meadow 20 acres; woodland 2 leagues long and one and a half leagues wide. Value before 1066 £4; later £3; now 100s. [£5].

Weddington
The Count of Meulan holds in Watitune 3 hides. Hereward holds from him; he also held it before 1066; he was free. In lordship one and a half ploughs and four slaves; 12 villagers and 5 smallholders with 4 ploughs. Meadow 20 acres; woodland 2 furlongs long and 1 furlong wide. Value 30s.

Chilvers Coton
Harold son of Earl Ralph holds Celverdestoche from the king. 8 hides. Land for 10 ploughs. In lordship half a plough and 9 slaves; 15 villagers and 7 smallholders with 7 ploughs. Meadow, 3 furlongs long and 1 wide; woodland a league and a half long and 1 league wide. The value was 40s; now 50s. His father held it.

This description of the local manors is very technical and not entirely comprehensible. The details concerning land tenure and use will be considered later, but the information on population size and social structure fills out the picture of the Anglo-Saxon vill. The entry for Etone lists 63 people in all. If these are taken to be heads of household, then the total population was in the range 250-300 people, allowing four to five persons per household. It is likely that just under half of this population lived in Attleborough, which on later evidence had slightly less arable land than the main vill, and that a few families lived in the woodlands of Stockingford. In that case, the vill of Etone at the Conquest was composed of some thirty households: 120-150 inhabitants. The three local manors list a total of 115 people, which would give a total population of under 600, compared with over 80,000 at the present day. Centuries after the first settlement the area was still very sparsely populated.

As regards social structure, the largest group in Ea-tun was the 44 villagers. These were the villeins or tenant-farmers holding on average a peasant farm of a yardland or virgate: some 25 to 30 acres of arable land. The 16 freedmen and smallholders were probably cottagers holding up to five acres of land, supplementing their incomes with craft or labouring work. The slaves belonged to the lord. They worked his demesne farm and are simply lumped in the account with his three ploughs. As for the manorial lords, Domesday Book shows both change and continuity. Harding, the Anglo-Saxon lord of Ea-tun and a group of estates in South Leicestershire, disappears from the record. Of the new Norman lord, Earl Aubrey of Northumbria, it was stated: 'of little use in difficult circumstances, he went home' to Normandy in the early 1080s. Hereward continued to hold Weddington but fell in status. No longer a free man, he held his manor as tenant of the Earl of Meulan, Robert de Beaumont. Only Chilvers Coton remained with its pre-1066 lord: Harold still held the

5   Church Street, west side, 1941. The massive chimney stacks and the timber framing exposed after the 17 May air raid show 17th-century houses behind the stucco rendering. The central building with its arched doorway became Lawyer Dempster's house in George Eliot's *Janet's Repentance*.

6   Church Street, 1906. The northern end of the street shows the onset of Edwardian re-development, with larger buildings, including the imposing *Queen's Head* public house (now the *Pen & Wig*), replacing earlier properties.

7 Bond Gate, post-1899. The northern end of the village was occupied by several farmhouses and enclosed crofts. The west side, with the 1899 Conservative Club in the foreground, remains largely unchanged from this photo but the buildings on the east side have all gone.

land of his father, Earl Ralph of Hereford, who was the nephew of the late King Edward.

Warwickshire Domesday Book has a second manor called Etone, held by Robert d'Oilly. This records a further 22 inhabitants with a total of 13 ploughs. Since Earl Aubrey's ploughlands correspond closely to later acreages for Nuneaton and Attleborough open fields, it is virtually impossible to fit this estate into Nuneaton. Robert's manor may have been Water or Wood Eaton in Oxfordshire, or a lost place in Ferncombe Hundred in southwest Warwickshire.

Working the Land: Medieval Farming

As well as land ownership, Domesday Book was also concerned with the economic value of each manor. Since for most manors wealth was expressed in agrarian terms, Domesday Book gives a detailed, though not easily understood, description of the state of local agriculture at the beginning of the Norman period.

In Ea-tun the lord had three ploughs on his demesne or home farm and the 44 villagers and 16 cottagers shared a further 16 ploughs. Here the plough represents not only the implement but also the plough team, conventionally of eight oxen, and the ploughing potential of the team: conventionally, again, a hundred acres. Thus Ea-tun, with a total of 19 ploughs, had some 1,900 acres of arable land in use, of which the lord farmed 300 acres and the men of the vill, including Attleborough, 1,600 acres. Since the 60 men of the two settlements were sharing 16 ploughs, it follows that, on average, each villager contributed a quarter of each plough team, that is two oxen. In return, he was able to work one quarter of a plough land, that is 25 acres. This 25-acre holding, known as a virgate or yardland, was the typical Midland peasant holding.

8 Back Street. Now part of the town's ring road, its ancient name indicates its original purpose: to give rear access to the village house plots. The two old cottages, part timber-framed, made way for a car park.

9 Horeston Fields. This aerial view shows the pattern of ridge and furrow strips of the open fields which covered all eastern Nuneaton. Part of the site of Horeston Grange, the priory's farming centre, appears bottom right.

The virgate was not a consolidated 25-acre block as on a modern farm. This is shown by a 13th-century deed which records a gift by Ralph Brian of Attleborough of seven acres of land there to Nuneaton Priory. Ralph's seven acres were made up of 15 separate half- and quarter-acre lots. The acre here is a unit of work: a day's ploughing. Anglo-Saxon farmers had found by trial and error that the most suitable distance to draw the heavy, wheel-less eight-ox plough was some 220 yards, the furlong or furrow length. In one day the plough team could cover this distance for a width of about 22 yards, making roughly an acre in all. This acre strip was ploughed in four sections, each some five and a half yards wide, with the soil heaped up into the centre of each section, leaving a furrow along each side. This ridge and furrow can still be seen where former arable land has later been put down to grass.

Ralph Brian's strips, then, were a furlong in length and either 11 or five and a half yards wide. Over the centuries the original acre strips had been subdivided, possibly between heirs or by sale or lease, until the basic unit had become the selion or land of a quarter-acre. These lands were grouped together in blocks known as furlongs, probably representing the original clearances, and the furlongs were, in turn, grouped into the two, three or more huge open fields necessary for crop rotation.

A survey of Chilvers Coton in 1684 describes how the three-field system still operated as it neared the end of a thousand years of continuity:

Windmill field bore Winter Corn and some Barly now this present year of our lord 1684, And will bear Beanes, Pease and Oates in 1685 and be fallow in 1686. Likewise Wamebrook field is fallow this year 1684 and will bear Winter Corn and some Barly in 1685 and Beanes Pease and Oates in 1686 and then fallow again. Also Greenemore field bore Beanes Pease and Oates in this year 1684 and will be fallow 1685 and will bear some Winter Corne and Barly in 1686 ... And after the Corn and Grass is taken away every one puts in Cattle according to his holdings, viz. He that holds a yardland four horses, Sixteen Beastes and Forty Sheep and so proportionably for a greater or lesser quantity ...

[Warwick CR 136, vol.109, p.73]

Nuneaton's three open fields were called Hollowbrook, Middle and Priesthill Fields; those of Attleborough were Paul's Ford, Middle and Wembrook Fields. All six fields ran roughly from the town and village outskirts across the wide, fertile plain to the eastern boundaries of the manor (Watling Street in Nuneaton's case). This was a huge expanse of open land, ridged and furrowed with grassy headlands for access to each furlong; treeless and hedgeless, except for the outer boundaries of each field. Only

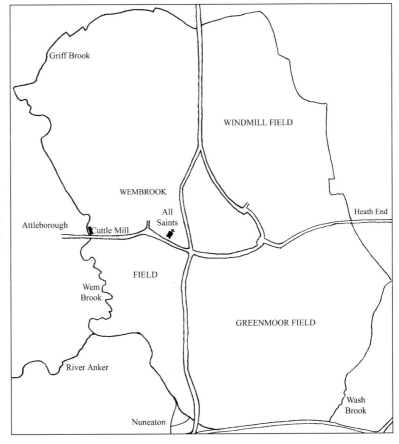

10 Chilvers Coton open fields in 1684. This plan is based on Robert Hewitt's map in the Newdigate Collection at Warwick County Record Office.

11 Bond Street, 1904. These two cottages were part of an early farmhouse which survived into the early 20th century, when they, with the *Crown* next door, were demolished to make way for the new *Crown Hotel*.

12 Bond Gate. Taken in the 1920s, this photograph shows Cracknell's blacksmith's shop, one of the last links with Nuneaton's farming past. The building, much altered, still survives.

two early buildings have been located inside this open field area: Horeston Grange and a windmill, both to the south-east of the modern Hinckley Road. Horeston was a moated farmhouse which was the centre for the demesne lands of Nuneaton Priory. These lands—the later Oaston Fields—were certainly enclosed and farmed as a separate unit by 1447.

The open fields did not, however, comprise the whole of the medieval farmlands. The farmers needed permanent grazing pasture and hay meadows which were usually found close to the river and streams. Meadow land was held in proportion to arable, usually an acre to a yardland, and allocated yearly by lot. Woodland provided timber, fencing materials, fuel and pasture, especially pannage for pigs. The western side of Nuneaton was extensively wooded though increasingly taken in and cleared during the medieval and Tudor periods.

13   Harefield Road: the cattle market. Though farming had long ceased to be a major part of the local economy, the town still served as an agricultural centre, the Tuesday cattle market surviving into the mid-1960s.

Known woods in 1543 include the Great Ley from Tuttle Hill to Caldecote, the Haunch Wood in Stockingford, and the Outwoods and Johns Wood covering the western part of Camphill. Lastly, there were stretches of common or waste land. Nuneaton had its commons to the west of Arbury Road and in the Whittleford–Bucks Hill area. Galley Common, as its name suggests, was largely waste. Its distinctive name came from Elinour Galley (died 1544) who lived in a cottage on the common. Chilvers Coton had its common in the area which is still called Heath End. These commons were only waste in the eyes of the manorial lords. For peasants they provided extra grazing and a source of fuel; for squatters, sites for cottages or hovels.

Most of the villeins in medieval Nuneaton had to rent their land from the lord of the manor, paying in cash and work services. In 1335 Nuneaton Priory set out the services paid by a typical tenant, Gilbert in Le Huyrne of Attleborough. Gilbert had a house and a yardland of 29 acres of arable and an acre of meadow. He paid a cash rent of two shillings a year plus a hen at Christmas and five eggs at Easter. In addition he had to plough, harrow, make hay, reap corn, cart dung and do other works on the priory's demesne lands at various times throughout the year. He had to give the priory first refusal when he had young beasts for sale, and when he died the priory could claim his best beast as a heriot before the kin could take over his farm. His sons could not enter the priesthood, nor his daughters marry outside the manor without the priory's permission so that their labour (and breeding potential!) would not be lost to the manor. No wonder that the street where many Nuneaton villeins had their farmhouses was called the Bond End. Gilbert and his fellows, their ancestors and descendants, were all tightly bound to the soil.

Two

THE PRIORY OF
ST MARY

By the early 12th century the manor of Eaton had passed to the Beaumont family, the powerful Earls of Leicester. In or about 1155, Robert Beaumont granted his manor of Eaton to the French Abbey of Fontevraud as the main endowment of a new daughter house in England. The order was unusual in that it comprised both nuns and monks, living apart, under the headship of the Abbess. As a daughter house headed by a prioress, Nuneaton was a priory, but contemporary documents call it 'abbatia' and the road leading to it seems always to be known as the Abbey End.

The priory builders found an ideal site on the lord's demesne land, half a mile west of the original vill. Here the ground dropped southwards to a stream running into the Anker. This enabled the builders to place the living quarters to the sheltered south of the priory church and have a water supply close by. The church was

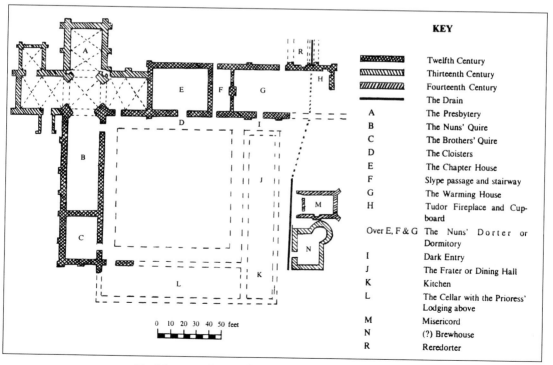

KEY

▨▨▨▨	Twelfth Century
▨▨▨▨	Thirteenth Century
▨▨▨▨	Fourteenth Century
	The Drain
A	The Presbytery
B	The Nuns' Quire
C	The Brothers' Quire
D	The Cloisters
E	The Chapter House
F	Slype passage and stairway
G	The Warming House
H	Tudor Fireplace and Cupboard
Over E, F & G	The Nuns' D o r t e r or Dormitory
I	Dark Entry
J	The Frater or Dining Hall
K	Kitchen
L	The Cellar with the Prioress' Lodging above
M	Misericord
N	(?) Brewhouse
R	Reredorter

0 10 20 30 40 50 feet

14 Nuneaton Priory: the church and monastic buildings.

cruciform in plan with a squat central tower over the crossing. The eastern section was the presbytery with the high altar. The nuns' quire occupied the crossing and the nave, except for the two western bays which were walled off to form the brothers' quire. One unusual feature was a lady chapel east of the north transept with access from a porch, suggesting that it was used by visitors and perhaps local people. When the Abbey Church was rebuilt in 1876 the remains of the tower piers were incorporated into the new structure, while the original west wall still stands close to Manor Court Road.

The domestic life of the priory was centred on the cloister, an open square some 135 feet across with covered alleys round its sides. The eastern cloister alley contained the night entrance into the church and gave access to the chapter house, a passage to the outer buildings and the nuns' parlour or warming house. The dorter or sleeping quarters, reached from a staircase in the passage, occupied the upper storey of this eastern range. Projecting eastwards was the two-storied reredorter or toilet block. Along the southern side of the cloister ran the refectory built over an undercroft with the kitchen in the south-west corner. The western range probably had the cellarium or storehouse on the ground floor with the prioress's private apartments above.

There were two free-standing rooms just south of the main block. One, with a circular appendage for a vat, was the brewhouse; the other a misericord, a small hall where nuns who wished could eat meat. Between these outer buildings and the southern range ran a covered culvert from the main stream which brought fresh water to the kitchen area. The drain then passed under the reredorter, washing waste and sewage back into the brook downstream of the priory, finally discharging into the Anker near the town mill.

No other outer buildings have been located but the Abbey Meadow, east of the main site, may be the site of the infirmary, almonry and a guest house. The brothers' house, later called the Habyte or Abbot's House, lay just to the west of the church and there are later references to houses, barns and stables in the west half of the precinct. On the western extremity of the site the stream had been dammed to make a pool—the Barpool—for a new priory mill. This 12-acre pool formed the western boundary of the priory precinct, the Barpool Brook the southern one. The eastern and northern sides were walled with a main gatehouse close to Abbey Green. The whole priory site covered some 34 acres.

The community seems to have flourished. The high point came in 1234 when there were 93 nuns in residence; a total maintained for nearly a century since there were still 89 nuns in 1328. By 1370, however, there were only 46 inmates. Forty new choir stalls were ordered in 1450, and a mere 25 nuns received pensions when the priory was dissolved in 1539. The office of prior disappeared after 1424, replaced by a lay Receiver-General, and the number of brethren, never reaching double figures, declined by 1539 to a single priest. Possibly the Black Death of 1348 onwards brought about the initial fall, but the long-term cause was most likely a waning enthusiasm for the monastic life.

We know little of the life led by the nuns. Apart from the daily round of services, the priory had to administer its large estates which extended into ten counties, to give charity to the poor, to nurse the sick, to teach girls seeking to enter the order and boys destined for the priesthood. Only occasionally did problems arise of sufficient importance to be recorded. One major difficulty was the upkeep of the priory itself. Shortly before 1234 the eastern piers supporting the central tower collapsed, leading to the rebuilding of the presbytery and both transepts. In 1237 and 1238 grants of oak trees were made from the royal forests towards the rebuilding. Within ten years a fire had destroyed other buildings and further oaks were given by the Bishop of Lichfield and Coventry from his forests at Cannock. Despite generous

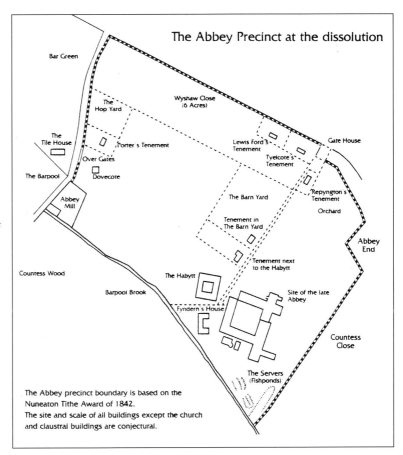

The Abbey Precinct at the dissolution

Bar Green

Wyshaw Close
(6 Acres)

The
Hop Yard

The
Tile House

Gate House

Porter's Tenement

Lewis Ford's
Tenement

Over Gates

Tyelcote's
Tenement

The Barpool

Dovecote

Repyngton's
Tenement

Abbey
Mill

The Barn Yard

Orchard

Tenement in
The Barn Yard

Abbey
End

Countess Wood

The Habytt

Tenement next
to the Habytt

Barpool Brook

Site of the late
Abbey

Fyndern's House

Countess
Close

The Servers
(Fishponds)

The Abbey precinct boundary is based on the
Nuneaton Tithe Award of 1842.
The site and scale of all buildings except the church
and claustral buildings are conjectural.

15 Nuneaton Priory: the precinct in the 16th century.

endowments the nuns were often short of money: in 1292 they complained that three or four times a week they lived on hard bread. Their plight was alleviated by capitalising on earlier gifts of church rectories. In 11 cases the priory installed a salaried vicar instead of a rector, keeping the balance of the great tithes as extra income.

The nuns themselves occasionally troubled the authorities. John of Gaunt, as successor to the founder, was much concerned with the shocking state of the priory in 1371 and handed over the administration to the Abbot of Leicester and three gentlemen. Perhaps John of Gaunt added to the priory's troubles that year by quartering there five Spanish ladies from the court. By August one lady was 'demorrant a Leycestre ovesque Johan Elmeshalle' and by December the Duke had heard '... que noz

damoisels d'Espagne demurrantz a Nouneton ne voullont pas illoeques pluis longement demerrer'. Scandal was rare but the Register of Bishop Gyrewell does recite that Joan Bruys, a nun of Nuneaton, had been abducted by Nicholas Green of Isham with whom she was living as his wife. More usual were accusations of mismanagement. One prioress, Matilda de Everingham, elected in 1448, was accused of extravagance and waste in 1461. She was pardoned in 1462 but dismissed from office in 1465. Despite the election of a new prioress, Matilda was acting as prioress in 1471 and again from 1486 until her death in 1500.

In 1447 the priory found itself in dispute with the vicar of Nuneaton and the freeholders and tenants of the town concerning rights of pasture in Horeston Field. This was ancient demesne land in the open fields which the

16 View of Nun-Eaton Nunnery in 1729. Nearly 200 years after its dissolution, most of the priory buildings were in ruins. This print by N. and S. Buck gives a fair, if somewhat inaccurate, impression of the nuns' choir to the right and the crossing arches.

17 Nuneaton Priory ruins, 1870. The few remains above ground provided a dramatic setting for a Victorian outing. Shortly afterwards excavation began for the building of a new abbey church.

priory had recently enclosed. The aggrieved parties had then thrown down the fences to gain access for their animals. Both sides agreed to the arbitration of Sir Edward Grey, Lord Ferrers of Groby. He was unable to resolve the conflicting claims but ordered the parties to seek a full examination of their claims. In 1453 the Abbot of Kenilworth, Richard Bosevyle vicar of Nuneaton, and prioress Matilda Everingham met in the house of one Roger Mulward of Nuneaton. Roger, who was over 80 years of age, swore on oath that 'for the time to which man's memory of the contrary does not stretch' Horeston Field had indeed been the private land of the priory and no other person had right of pasture over it. Roger's long memory of how things had been was sufficient to decide the case against the vicar and the townsmen.

There is a good local example of living conditions inside a monastery. The Sudeley family, lords of Chilvers Coton, had endowed a small priory of Augustinian canons with land, and a monastery was built around 1155 close to the site of the present Arbury Hall. This priory, like so many others, was short of ready cash so, to supplement its income, it offered corrodies or pensions to lay people. For a sum of money paid in advance, the priory would offer board and lodging for life—a primitive and risky form of annuity. Though beneficial to the priory in the short term, pensioners did tend to outlive their cash payment and become a burden on already over-stretched finances. A deed of 1485 lists the terms of such a pension granted by Arbury Priory to William and Agnes Elys of Coventry. The pensioners were provided with housing, food, fuel, light and transport. The major items of food were 24 pounds of bread and 80 pints of ale weekly, a reminder that bread was the staple food before potatoes and ale the only safe drink. The pensioners could also obtain cooked food from the prior's kitchen and bring in their own food for cooking. For this pension, William and Agnes paid one hundred marks; well over £5,000 in modern money. The main provisions of the agreement were as follows:

> a mancion with a hall of stage, the howsys and chambers perteyning to the same … sufficiently reparyd with the costys and charges of the said prior and convent and so continually to be maynteynyd and kepyd during the term aforesaid.

> Also 8 loves of the convent brede and 4 loves of the secund brede wekely, every love weyng too pondes.

> Also 8 galons of the best ale and too galons of the secund ale.

> Also in kechyn at every meyle of every dyett als moche as too chanons have.

> And yf the said William and Agnes have any manner of mete, Fysshe or flesche besyd, hyt to be dyrte in the prior's kechyn at the priors coste.

> Also barbor and launder.

> Also 6 lodys of herdwood sufficiently brokn and dressyd accordyng to there chymnes.

> Also 100 fagotes with a howse to kepe there wod dry yn …

> Also 20 lb of tallow candull yerly with half a stryke of salte.

> Also gras for too kyne wynter and somer.

> Also the kepyng of too horses on in severell gras …

> Also yerely 6 cheses price 2d apece.

[extract from P.R.O. Calendar of Ancient Deeds B 1498]

Similar corrody houses existed at Nuneaton Priory as well. In general, the presence of lay people not bound by conventual rules had a distracting and occasionally destructive effect on life within monasteries.

18 St Mary's Abbey Church, Manor Court Road. The architects tried to reproduce faithfully the monastic church. The Norman-style nave was built in 1876 and the medieval chancel in 1906. The north transept dates from 1930, after this photo was taken.

Town Development

Ea-tun at the time of the Domesday Survey was a village east of the Anker. Its main source of livelihood was farming and allied crafts, its size and importance little greater than that of neighbouring vills. The foundation of the priory marked the beginning of change. Firstly, the village began to be named Nuneaton to differentiate it from the many other places by water called 'Eaton'. More importantly, the manor was the priory's chief endowment and its exploitation was essential if the priory was to be financially secure. The priory, then, set out to develop Nuneaton and, by so doing, changed it from a village into a town.

The first step was to obtain a royal grant for a weekly market, which King Henry II granted around 1160. At a time when shops were almost unknown, most trading had to be done in open market and the grant of this right was a royal prerogative. The market was first held on Sunday after mass, probably in the churchyard or close by. The close proximity of ancient markets to parish churches has been noted. In Nuneaton's case, the east side of the river was already fully taken up by the existing village so, when a market place became necessary, it had to be sited on the west bank of the river on the demesne land of the priory. The most suitable

site proved to be the junction of the road to Coventry with the one to Atherstone (now Abbey Street). A large rectangular place was laid out stretching from the river crossing towards Wash Lane (now Queen's Road) and reaching back to the north side of the Atherstone Road. Trades and craftsmen would tend to occupy plots round this new market place so beginning expansion beyond the limits of the original village. In 1226 King Henry III confirmed the original grant of the market, changing the day to Tuesday. The king once more confirmed his grant in 1232, finally changing the day to Saturday:

> Henry by the grace of God king of England, Duke of Normandy and Aquitaine and Count of Anjou to Archbishops, Bishops, Priors, Earls, Barons, Justices, Sheriffs, Reeves, ministers, and all Bailiffs and his faithful [subjects] greeting. Know ye that we have granted and by this our charter have confirmed for us and our heirs to god and the Church of the Blessed Mary at Ethon and to the Prioress and nuns there serving God, that they may have and hold in perpetuity one market every week on Saturday, which [market] is accustomed to be held every week on Tuesday provided that the market may not be to the harm of neighbouring markets ... Given at Feckenham on the second day of June in the 17th year of our Reign. [2 June 1232]

[British Library Add. Ch. 48494]

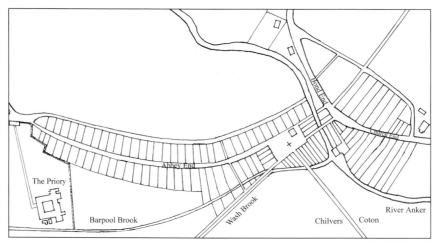

19   Medieval Nuneaton, *c.*1350. The Market Place and Abbey Street were a new town grafted on to the original village. The plots are conjectural and not to scale.

20 Newdegate Square, pre-1914. The projecting wing of the old *Newdegate Arms* was once Nuneaton Priory's moot or court hall. Originally free-standing, it became incorporated by the 17th century in the *Crown Inn* which stood behind it.

As well as the market, Henry II made a further grant around 1163 to the priory of an annual fair on the feast of Holy Cross (3 May) and the four following days. A fair was a much more important event than the weekly market: the latter only attracted custom from the surrounding villages, while fairs were much rarer and brought both traders and customers from a much wider area. In 1239 Henry III also confirmed this grant and added the two days preceding the feast. For a whole week the market place would be crowded with traders who went from fair to fair across the country and with customers from a wide area around the town.

The priory used the market and fair to augment its income by charging rent for stalls (stallage) and by exacting tolls on goods coming

21 Market Place: the cross. The medieval market cross, surmounted by an octagonal chamber, was on the site now occupied by the fountain. The bell was rung to signal the start of trading. This sketch from the *Nuneaton Diary* was made before the edifice was pulled down in 1810.

22 Bridge Street, 1907. The earliest river crossing was probably further north, running from Abbey Street through to Wheat Street. Bridge Street probably developed with the establishment of the medieval market place. Much of the north side remains, but ill-conceived road widening swept away the south side and much of the street's character.

into the market place. Until modern redevelopment, all the entrances into the market place were very narrow—a practical measure against toll evasion. The existence of a market and fair—privileges possessed by none of the surrounding villages—made Nuneaton the economic centre of the area, giving it the pre-eminence which it still enjoys. As the main trading place, Nuneaton would also attract traders and craftsmen into the town, increasing its population, and thus the rent income to the priory, and changing its occupational structure from mainly farming to that of a mixed agrarian-trading economy.

The priory also took positive steps to attract newcomers to the town by offering land and privileges to potential buyers. These are detailed in a charter of around 1227 in which the priory offered quite generous conditions to

people taking up those new burgage plots on offer in the town:

To all Christ's faithful people to whom this present writing shall come Sibilla, Prioress, and Richard, Prior, of Eton and the whole Convent of the same place give eternal greetings in the Lord. Know ye that we by our universal consent have given and granted to our burgesses of Eton, to all that is who have taken burgages in that vill to be held of us, or those who will in the future, that they may have and hold the same burgages of us to themselves and their heirs for ever, well, in peace and freely, with the same liberty as the burgesses of Coventry hold their burgages of the Prior himself in Coventry, rendering thence annually for each burgage 15d for all service and demands pertaining to the said burgage, at the three terms of the year, namely: at the feast of St. Michael 5d, at the Purification of

Blessed Mary 5d, and at Pentecost 5d. And be it known that every single burgage shall measure 9 perches in length and 3 in width. But if any burgage shall have more or less than the full burgage according to the aforesaid measure, then each shall pay rent for the size of his holding …

[British Library Add. Ch. 48490]

These burgage plots were freehold properties, the only charge being the chief rent of 15d. yearly which was paid instead of the services demanded by the priory from its farming tenants. The plot dimensions given in the charter mean a frontage of 50 feet and a depth of 150 feet. Most of these new plots

23 & 24 Market Place. *Above*, looking west, pre-1909. *Below*, looking east, *c*.1904. After Nuneaton gained a charter, a market place was laid out west of the river.

25   Market Place, looking east, *c*.1911.

are to be found in Abbey Street where the
north side still contains many properties whose
frontage is 50 feet or a factor of that amount:
25 or 75 feet. The chief rents laid down in
1227 demonstrate this long continuity. They
were still being collected by the lords of the
manor as late as 1780. Abbey Street in 1227
came into being in a way similar to a modern housing estate. The land along the road
from the new market place up to the priory
precinct wall was divided into quite regular
plots and offered for sale. Burgage Walk marks
the rear boundary of the plots on the northern side and there may have been a similar
lane to the south.

The word 'burgage' is significant in that
it is usually connected with voting rights and
a measure of self-government. The charter
declares that burgage holders in Nuneaton were
to have the same rights and privileges as the
burgesses of the Prior of Coventry had in that
city. This is the usual medieval formula for
detailing rights; perfectly clear to contem-
poraries but unfortunately quite obscure today.
However, Tudor evidence shows that the
priory's scheme to attract new freemen was
not a complete success. No more than half the
possible freehold plots seem to have been taken
up by prospective freeholders; the rest being
let on a yearly tenancy. Neither did Nuneaton

26 Burgage Walk, 1970. This began as the back lane when Abbey Street was developed following the grant of burgage rights by the priory around 1227. It marked the northern extent of the built-up part of the town centre almost into the 20th century.

27 Abbey Street, looking east, pre-1914. All the properties on the north side have similar size frontages, showing that they occupy earlier burgage plots.

28 Abbey Street, looking east, *c*.1908. Many of the north-side properties have survived, but much has changed, including the former *Half Moon*. The Methodist church spire (1881) stands out on the Stratford Street corner.

become a seignorial borough with its own mayor and corporation. Owing to the low take-up of plots, the rights of the burgesses were not fulfilled. Again, the often quoted statement that Nuneaton sent members to the parliament of 1275 seems to be without foundation since no representatives for the town have been traced in the published rolls of Commons' membership.

The greatest change that can be ascribed to the priory's influence is on the physical plan of the town. Market Place and Abbey Street were, in fact, a new town grafted on to the ancient Anglo-Saxon vill. The centre of Nuneaton had crossed the River Anker and Market Place, with its market cross and manor court or moot hall, had become the heart of the town. The parish church of St Nicolas was left, almost stranded, on the outskirts of the town. This is in striking contrast to most medieval town plans, where church and market stand in close proximity.

Three

MEDIEVAL PEOPLE,
CHURCHES AND MANOR HOUSES

By the early 14th century it is possible to find documents which refer to actual living townspeople and so begin the reconstruction of their lives and work. In 1327, and again in 1332, parliament granted a Lay Subsidy to the king. This was a tax of one-fifteenth (one-tenth in corporate towns) of the value of personal and household goods. Only the more wealthy inhabitants—probably about a third of all householders—were taxed and there must have been many attempts at under-assessment and even evasion. These two early rolls, however, are very valuable since they contain lists of taxpayers, providing the first, although incomplete, population listings for the town.

There are 68 names listed for Nuneaton in the 1332 tax roll. This suggests that the town with its hamlets of Attleborough and Stockingford would have some 200 households, compared with the 63 calculated from Domesday Book. These figures are obviously very approximate but the trend is quite clear. The priory's development of the town had paid dividends with something like a three-fold increase in occupants. It is likely that this tax roll represents a high point in the growth of the medieval population. In the early summer of 1349 the Black Death reached the Midlands and, if national mortality estimates are at all reliable, the total population may have been at least a third lower by the end of the century. For Nuneaton it is certain that the growth evident up to 1332 was not sustained. Quite

reliable evidence in 1543 for Nuneaton town alone suggests some 176 households and just over 800 inhabitants. This appears to indicate an absolute decline before 1400 with a slow recovery over the next century and a half.

The Lay Subsidy rolls of 1327 and 1332 and a View of Frankpledge (manor court proceedings) of 1344 give three sets of names within a period of 17 years which can be used to provide a fuller picture of work in, and migration to, 14th-century Nuneaton. Of 172 listed surnames, 42 give some indication of trade or occupation. Six names refer to an official position within the priory manor: bailiff, park keeper, forester, watchman and two court officials, summoner and messenger. Then there are nine service trades which would be found in most small market towns: apothecary, barber, shop keeper, carpenter, painter, miller, blacksmith, carter and horse keeper. More significantly, 12 names show the rise of manufacturing trades in the town. These reflect locally available raw materials which are by-products of farming: wood, wool and leather. As well as the carpenter, wood trades are represented by a cart wright and turners. Textile workers include shearman, dyer and tailors. The largest group is the leather trade. Tanner and cobbler are the obvious occupations; more specialised are bag and purse makers and sadlers. The two final occupations are button maker and mat (or mattress) maker. Farmers are not specifically named in the lists but there are shepherd, swineherd and a dairy maid employed in agriculture. Some five names—Cours, Godhiue, Halle, Page and Sweyn—describe servants, and the priory would have been a major source of employment in both domestic and maintenance work. In all, the names show the increasingly complex local economy as Nuneaton slowly transformed itself from a village into a town.

One factor to influence the increasing spread of occupations must have been migration. Thirty-seven surnames derive from identifiable places outside Nuneaton manor. As might be expected, most migrants have travelled less than fifty miles, but seven names do refer to places a considerable distance from the town. At least three of these distant places—Muresley in Buckinghamshire, Amesbury in Wiltshire and Beddington in Surrey—had connections with the priory, so the presence of settlers from them is not beyond possibility. Nearly 25 per cent of the listed surnames derive from places outside the manor of Nuneaton. In spite of attempts by lords to tie tenants to manors, there seems to have been a considerable amount of movement from place to place, sometimes involving migration over quite long distances. The often repeated statement that peasants rarely left their manor, living their lives in the one place, is open to question, even at this early period.

The influence of the priory over the town extended far beyond economic development; it also exerted a considerable control over the lives of the inhabitants. As the manorial lord of Nuneaton, the priory had the right to hold the manor court which met in the court hall situated in the north-east corner of the Market Place. The court acted as a primitive form of local council, making by-laws and regulations affecting the economic, agrarian and social life of the town. The priory had also acquired the right to hear minor cases usually tried by the shire or royal courts. This latter function was known as a View of Frankpledge and one typical View—that of the court held on Tuesday

6 April 1344—adds another dimension to our knowledge of life in the medieval town.

The manor of Nuneaton was divided up into tithings. Originally these had been groups of ten families, each group choosing one head as its tithing man. He acted as an unpaid constable who was responsible for the good conduct of his own and the other nine families. To ensure that the tithing men actually carried out their sometimes unpopular tasks, the jury— the 12 men representing the collective wisdom and knowledge of the manor—had the duty of reporting recalcitrant tithing men to the manor court.

> The Jurors say that John Gamel (fined 2d) is harbouring strangers against the assize, therefore he is in mercy. And because the tithing man across the water [i.e. east of the river] has concealed this (2d) therefore he is in mercy.
>
> [British Library Add. Roll 49522]

In such a localised society, tithing men were a feasible method of control. The apprehending of offenders was similarly a corporate action. When an offence was committed, witnesses raised a hue and cry, shouting and chasing after the offender, followed by all who heard the cry. If the alarm were justified the offender was duly fined. There are ten such cases presented at the 1344 court. In three further cases, hue and cry was raised unjustly (possibly maliciously) and the person who called out the town was fined instead:

> Likewise they present that Deonisia le Wayte has raised hue and cry justly upon John Heynote, clerk (2d). Therefore he is in mercy, pledge Richard de Burton.
>
> Likewise they present that Lucia Hebbe (2d) has raised hue and cry unjustly upon Richard de Greneburgh.

The most frequent offences before the court were concerned with the water courses or ditches which ran through the town, especially digging up, obstructing or erecting privies upon them. Nineteen persons were found guilty (in mercy) of these and similar offences. Medieval Nuneaton also appears to have been a violent place. There are 13 cases of fighting, some involving women. In each case the parties had pledges, persons responsible for the attendance of the parties in court. In six cases one party failed to appear and the guarantors were also fined. The last main type of offence was harbouring strangers, or unreported newcomers as yet outside manorial jurisdiction. The following extracts from the court roll all come from the tithing 'this side the water', that is the Market Place and Abbey End area:

> They came with two tithing men namely William de Quteley and Richard de Gildeford. And they present that they give for the common fine 2s. Also they present that William Hereward (3d) and Thomas Boseuill (1d) have erected a privy on the common river bank to the hurt [of the public] And an order is made that it should be redressed. Like wise they present that John de Peystelton (1d) and Roger le Wrytesone (2d) are stopping up the ditch at brocherbrugge with ashes therefore they are in mercy And an order is made … Likewise they present that Robert Sadler of Higham (1d) has made a privy at the great bridge on the river bank to the hurt [of the public] … And it presented that Anabill Hobbe (1d) is harbouring strangers against the assize therefore she is in mercy … Also they present that Agnes Loteman (2d) has drawn blood from Elisabeth de Mancestre. Therefore she is in mercy, pledge Geoffrey Materasmakere. And the said Geoffrey (1d) does not have the said Agnes therefore he is in mercy … Also they present that Thomas Say (3d) has drawn blood from John son of Roger Christiane.

The second part of the court record concerns the assize of ale. Each tithing had two ale tasters whose duties consisted of checking the quality, quantity and price of ale and reporting illegal brewing. Three people are charged as regrators, who buy ale and then resell at a higher price. The vast majority of cases—some 75 at this one court—refer to brewing before the assize, that is without prior permission. It seems likely that these brewers

29 The Town Bridge. In 1335 the priory bailiffs received a grant of pontage—tolls for repair—levied on all goods passing over Nuneaton Bridge. That bridge was swept away in a great mid-16th-century flood. Its successor, shown here, was changed beyond recognition when commercial premises were built over the south side.

were presented not with the intention of stamping out such brewing but to impose a tax on all brewing within the manor. The existence of so many brewers in such a small town emphasises the dubious quality of the local water supply, inextricably linked to sewage disposal, and suggests a reason for the high level of violence with which the court is concerned!

The final entry on the court roll is of considerable interest. Thomas, son of Simon le Meleward, who is described as a villein of the priory, is permitted to take holy orders. Monasteries were often ready to put forward suitable boys to the priesthood, but the advancement of a villein would mean the loss of his manpower to the manor:

30 Attleborough Square. Hall End, Lutterworth Road, Bull Street and Kem Street once surrounded an open village green. The buildings on the left are later encroachments on this green. Many properties in the centre and on the right survive to give Attleborough the feel of a real village.

To this court ... came Thomas, son of Simon le Meleward of Herbury, clerk, and villein of the prioress and convent of Eton before Brother John de Wappenbury, then Prior of Eton, and he petitioned for a licence from the said Lord Prior that he might be given a tonsure by the Bishop without dispute. And the aforesaid Lord Prior of his special grace and charity in the name of the said Prioress and convent gave him licence that when the time seems fit he may properly receive from the Bishop a tonsure and all other holy orders without the dispute of the said Prioress, Prior and convent or any servants in their name ...

In Dugdale's list of the chaplains of the chantry of St Mary in Bedworth parish church there appears one Thomas White *alias* Milleward, admitted to office on 1 August 1393. It is possible that both entries refer to the same person. In 1344 Thomas was a boy about to enter the priesthood; nearly fifty years later, towards the end of his life, he took on the barely onerous duties of priest to a small under-endowed chantry.

Though an Anglo-Saxon church in Nuneaton is only a possibility, there is good evidence for a church here in the late-Norman period. Before 1118 the manor had passed to Robert Beaumont, Count of Meulan and Earl of Leicester, who granted the rectory of his church at Eaton to the Norman Abbey of Lyre. This church must have existed before 1155, when Robert's son obtained King Henry II's confirmation of the earl's gift.

Nothing of the fabric of this Norman church survives. The earliest parts of the present St Nicolas Church date from around 1340, mainly in the south chapel arcade, so it seems likely that the church was rebuilt about

31   Chilvers Coton, Bridge Street, 1930s. The village, bisected first by the railway and later by the dual carriageway, seems to have had two centres. The lower, round the later railway arches, extended from near All Saints Church to Bridge Street. The old cottages to the right made way for the present traffic island.

32   Chilvers Coton, the Bull Ring. The upper part centres on the Bull Ring and Virgin's End (College Street)—both names remain obscure. Goode's butcher's shop (later Evans') bore the date 1756. The old house to the right has fortunately been preserved; at its rear was Coton Foundry.

33 & 34 *Above*, St Nicolas parish church. To the north stood the old Grammar School and the parish almshouses on the edge of the churchyard. *Left*, the interior, which shows the church before the 1965 restoration, when the galleries above both aisles were removed and the walls whitened. Just visible is the cut in the tower wall which marks the original pitched roof before the clerestory and the magnificent oak ceiling were added in the late 15th century.

this time. This coincides with the rise in population which peaked in the 1340s. The mid-14th-century church had a western tower, nave and a chancel, with chapels on its north and south sides. The north aisle was probably built at this time; possibly the southern aisle as well. The nave had a gabled roof which can still be traced by a chase cut in the interior (east) wall of the tower. With its low roof and the main windows in the aisles, it must have been a rather dark building. The chancel and eastern chapels were separated from the main body of the church by the rood screen, marked today only by an exterior stair tower on the south wall.

Towards the end of the 15th century this medieval church was drastically remodelled. The pitched roof was taken off and the nave walls raised to allow for eight tall clerestory windows on each side. The effect must have been dramatic. Obscurity gave way to light. The new low-pitched roof over the nave and both aisles had a wooden ceiling with carved bosses at its many intersections. These bosses are the great glory of the church: a marvellous mixture of royal and religious symbols, grotesque faces and naturalistic foliage. The walls, too, were painted with religious themes. Two of these were uncovered and recorded in 1837: a wheel of life dated 1515 and a skeleton with biblical quotations concerning death.

The last pre-Reformation change took place in 1507. John Leke of Nuneaton had endowed a chantry chapel where a priest would offer masses for the souls of the founder and his family. The chantry was sited in the south-east chapel, the change being marked by two 16th-century windows between, and at a higher level than, the existing pair. Local wills of the 1530s and 1540s give a little more information about the church interior. In addition to the high altar, there are references to the Lady, St Ann and Jesus altars and to St Catherine's Chapel. An inventory of church goods made in the reign of Edward VI lists furnishings and vestments:

Nuneton

Item there oon chalice and 3 belles, 3 vestments oon velvet two silke with th'appurtenances, a sute of vestments Sayes for deacon and subdeacon, a cope of satyn red, two corporys cases velvet, two pillowes, 3 altar clothes, 4 towells whereof oon diaper, a paire of sensers, a paire of organes, 3 Iles covered with led.

Memorandum that the parishe have solde since the begynning of the Kings Majesties Reigne to the reparacion of the highwaies, to th'alteracion of their church and suts for a free schoole there which is now established by our said Soveraigne for ever, theis parcelles folowing:

A cope of red velvet, a sute of vestments wulsted, a cope wulsted. A crosse bras, two candlesticks latyne.

Because Nuneaton St Nicolas was such a large parish, stretching some six miles from Bramcote north-westwards to Ansley, there was need to provide for the outlying hamlets. Attleborough had a medieval chapel possibly situated on the Freer Street corner of the Green. This fell into disuse in the later 16th century, after which time the inhabitants were expected to worship at St Nicolas. The canons of St Mary de Pre in Leicester, who owned an estate in Stockingford, had a chapel there. Nothing is known of its history but a Galley Common field-name—Chapell Yard 1690—hints at its possible site.

The other two ancient parish churches have both suffered destruction and rebuilding. All Saints Chilvers Coton, largely destroyed by enemy action on 17 May 1941, still retains most of its 13th-century chancel and a 15th-century tower. In its medieval form it had a tower, nave, chancel and a south-eastern chapel. St James Weddington was rebuilt in brick in 1733 but an early 14th-century stone north transept still survives. Both churches are listed in the Edwardian inventory:

Chilvers Coton

Item there oon chalice and 2 belles in the steple, a cope silke, 2 vestments oon silke, two old surpleses.

Memorandum that the parishe have solde
sithence the last survey oon broken bell to the
mending of highwaies and reparacions of their
church.

Weddington
Item there oon chalice and oon bell, two old
vestments, a surples, an altar clothe, a corporys,
a case thereto.

Nuneaton's manor house would have fallen
into disuse when the manor was granted to
St Mary's Priory, which now exercised the
function of manorial lord. There was a manor
house in Weddington about which little is
known, and any building there was lost with
the erection of the Victorian Weddington Castle.
Chilvers Coton, on the other hand, had two
manor houses in the medieval period.

For some three centuries after the
Conquest, Chilvers Coton remained in the
possession of the Sudeley family of Gloucester-
shire, descendants of the Earl Ralph whose son
held the manor in Domesday Book. In the late
12th century, Ralph de Sudeley alienated most
of his possessions in Chilvers Coton and Griff
to the church by founding a priory of
Augustinian canons at Arbury and also a cell of
the order of Knights Templar. He did,
however, retain the manor house at Griff and
its associated lands. This house, excavated in
1966, stood towards the southern point of the
triangle formed by the Nuneaton-Coventry
railway line, Griff Lane and the Bermuda Arm
of the Coventry Canal, occupying a two-acre
site bounded by a wide, shallow moat.

35 Chilvers Coton church and vicarage. Only the tower remains of this charming view. The vicarage was
demolished in the early 1930s and the church was largely destroyed in the air raid on 17 May 1941. Both featured
strongly in George Eliot's *Scenes of Clerical Life*.

Two main stages of construction have been identified by excavation. In the first, the manor house consisted of a hall, 38 x 20 feet, a fore-chamber and a small external room, probably the chapel. Since two pillar bases were discovered along the centre line of the hall floor, the building must have been two-storied. In the second stage of building, a large chamber 24 x 14 feet to the north of the hall and a second external room—most probably a garderobe (lavatory)—were added. There were traces of other buildings within the moated area but these had been badly disturbed by later coal mining and by ploughing.

Archaeological evidence dates occupation to between c.1280 and c.1380. The latter date fits in well with the transfer of ownership to Thomas le Bottiller of Wem, Shropshire, in 1380 and the probable abandonment of a separate manor house at Griff. There is documentary evidence, however, for earlier occupation than 1280, since between 1231 and 1242 the third Ralph de Sudeley was given the following licence:

> Hugh, Prior, and the Convent of Arbury grant to Ralph de Sudeley 'our patron' the right to have Mass celebrated in his chapel of Griff by his own private chaplain. The Prior of Arbury and the Vicar of Chilvers Coton are not to be obliged to celebrate Mass there, nor give material assistance in the way of candles, books or vessels. It is to be celebrated only when Ralph or his heirs, or their wives, are present in person, but not at the main feast days of the year ... The priest who celebrates in this chapel is to take oath that he will restore to the Vicar of Chilvers Coton all offerings he receives in the chapel. He shall exact no tithes of any sort, and on feast days he shall receive no parish-ioner of the mother church in the chapel.
>
> [Summary of licence]

As well as founding Arbury Priory, the first Ralph de Sudeley made a gift of the Griff-Bermuda area of his manor to the Knights Templar. The Templars were a military order charged with the protection of pilgrims in the Holy Land. An international order, they enjoyed great popularity and power, acting as bankers for European kings. Such power led to their downfall. Between 1307 and 1312 the order was suppressed by the Pope, and their English lands passed briefly to the Crown before being re-granted to the Order of St John of Jerusalem (the Hospitallers). From the brief period of royal control, Exchequer accounts give a glimpse of life on a local manor during the medieval period.

It is most unlikely that any of the Knights actually lived at the Griff manor house since one of their main preceptories was at Temple Balsall, some fifteen miles away. The Chilvers Coton manor provided income from rents, crops and stock. It lay immediately south-west of the later Bermuda village. As at Sudeley, the remains were very fragmentary, much disturbed by later coal mining, but the foun-dations of the hall have been traced by excavation and there is documentary evidence for a chamber and a chapel.

The Exchequer accounts for 1309 show the poor state of this manor. The income amounted to £4 6s. 1½d., mainly rents paid by the tenants but also including the sale of 'sea coal' which brought in 10s. 6d. This is the earliest reference to coal mining in the area, earlier than the 1275 date given in the *Victoria County History* vol.II. The income, in fact, did not quite meet expenditure. The largest single item was wages. The manor house employed seven farm workers and a boy who were paid 18s. 4d. for the year, with another 5s. 3¼d. for threshing grain and peas. The chaplain 'celebrating divine service for the souls of the ancestors and descendants of John de Sudlee' was paid 23s. 6d. for 18 weeks and four days.

The property was in need of repair, since 4s. 6d. had to be spent on ridge tiles and lime and the wages of a roofer and boy. Buying in of grain and peas for household use and sowing and other small sundry items completed the account.

On 24 June 1309 there was a royal visitor at the late Templars' Griff manor. King

Edward II stayed overnight on his way to Chester to meet Piers Gaveston, the royal favourite, returning from exile in Ireland. The poor state of this house is emphasised by the lengthy repairs needed to make it habitable for the royal visit. The accounts suggest it was a timber-framed building with lath and plaster infilling.

Chelvescote
The same [accountant] renders account of 6s. 8d. from the sale of branches felled there for the repair of the chamber ... and of £6 13s. 4d.

received from the King's Treasury by the hands of Alexander le Peintur

Expenses
The same reckons spent on the expenses caused by the repair and improvement of the King's Chamber as: on the wage of one carpenter and his mate for 6 weeks on laths, nails, tiles, lime and sand bought for the same together with

the wages of one roofer spending a month on the roofing of the same   21s. 5½d.

and on wooden vessels made from the king's own timber
1 iron tripod bought
1 wooden bucket for carrying water bought together with
1 bushel of rye bought for the household pottage   15d.

Stock
The same renders account of 12 pigs sent for the King there as a present and delivered to the same Keeper by the steward of the King's household.

From the dating of royal writs issued *en route*, the King probably left London about 21 June 1309, stayed at Chilvers Coton on the 24th, and arrived at Chester on 27 June. On the return journey the King stayed at Merevale Abbey and at Coventry while passing through this area.

Four

The End of Monastic Rule

By the beginning of the 16th century Nuneaton Priory was already in a state of decline. Even as early as 1459, when Thomas Karver of Lichfield was employed to make new choir stalls for the priory, only 40 were needed. The decline was to continue; there were only 15 nuns by 1507. The main reason for reduced numbers is a falling off in the religious vocation. The communal monastic life became less favoured among wealthier Catholics than the individual fervour of the *devotio moderna*, or the private family religion of the chantry chapel with its emphasis on the salvation of departed souls. Not only was there a falling off in vocation among Catholics but there was also increasing criticism and hostility from Protestant elements in the population which was seized upon by many Tudor gentry envious of monastic possessions and wealth.

During the years leading up to the annulment of Henry VIII's marriage to Katherine of Aragon, the monasteries came increasingly under attack. Among the Letters and Papers of Henry VIII is this letter from Sir Walter Smyth, sheriff of Warwickshire and Leicestershire:

Walter Smyth to Thomas Cromwell:
I moved you of a priory near me called Nuneaton, that keeps no good rule either to God or the world: for one of the nuns is with child now, and all the country is surprised, the convent being a house of such great lands. Please move the king in this matter that, as he is founder, there may be a new prioress, and his Grace shall have £100 for his lawful favour and you shall have £40 for yourself: and thus

doing you may have thanks of God and the world. Let me know your pleasure by the bearer.

Schenford, 30th September [1533]

The letter is as remarkable for what it omits as for what it actually says. Having made the accusation of immorality, Smyth offers neither names or details. The locality is surprised not because the priory is a religious house but because of its great property. In fact, property is at the heart of the letter. If the prioress is removed, the king as successor to the founder will expect payment for approving her successor, Thomas Cromwell, as vicar-general, will claim fees for the new election and Smyth will have gained favour at court. The allegation does not seem to have been pursued and Agnes Olton, the prioress accused in the letter, remained in office until the convent was finally dissolved six years later.

In 1536 Henry VIII ordered the closure of all the smaller monastic houses whose income was below £200 per annum. Given the declining monastic population, this can be seen as a sensible rationalisation. One of the dissolved houses was Arbury Priory, valued at £100 5s. 5¼d., which only had seven brothers: 'All of good lyving and desier yf the house be cepressed to be sent to some other house of ther religion'. Arbury Priory and its lands passed to Charles Brandon, Duke of Suffolk and brother-in-law of the king. Nuneaton Priory, with a gross income of £290 15s. 0½d., survived this first round of closures.

In February 1538 a second letter reached Thomas Cromwell, this time pleading for Nuneaton Priory. The writer was Cecily, wife of Lord Dudley, 'a weak man of understanding' who had fallen into poverty. Begging help from the King and trusting Cromwell to further her cause, she continued:

> The truth is I have little above twenty pounde a yere which I have by my lady my mother to find me and oone of my doghters with a woman and a man to wayte upon me and surely onless for the good Pryorys of Nuneton dyd give me meate and drynke of free cost to me and all myne that here remaynes with me I colde not tell what shyft to make. And besides that whensoever any of my children comes hether to see me they be welcome unto the pryorys as long as they lyst to tarry horse meate and mans meate and cost them nothing with a pece of gold or two in there purses at there departure. Wherefore I desire you to be goode lord unto me and consider the povertie of me for if oughte shulde come to the house of Nuneton I stand in a hard case.

Since Cecily's nephew Thomas, Lord Marquis of Dorset, was the Chief Seneschal of the priory, she had a strong claim on the nuns' charity. The hospitality and the gold given to her children was more liberal than the 12s. of corn given to the poor at the priory gate every week.

Cecily's letter did not influence the royal will. When the King ordered the dissolution of all remaining monasteries, in 1539, Nuneaton did not escape. On 12 September 1539 Dr John London, one of Thomas Cromwell's commissioners, received the deed of surrender sealed by the prioress and marked with 27 crosses. After nearly four hundred years the priory, which had shaped and controlled life in the town, ceased to exist.

Little is known of the subsequent fate of the ex-nuns. Agnes Olton found a lodging at the collegiate church of St Mary Astley, where the small community of chantry priests escaped dissolution until November 1545. Agnes' life in the world, however, proved only to be of short duration since she died at Astley on 2 August 1540. Only one other nun has appeared in local documents: Isabel Purefey was, in 1543, the tenant of a house in the Market Place. Seventeen former nuns were still drawing their pensions in 1553.

Henry VIII's instructions to the dissolution commissioners were quite explicit and very efficient. All valuables were to be removed for the King's use. Inventories of goods seized were

36 Market Place: old houses. This 1891 sketch shows the town we have lost. These three houses were replaced by Moon's and Clay's shops. In 1543 former nun Isabel Purefey occupied one of these cottages. The middle house bears the name Astley, possibly John Astley, the author of the *Nuneaton Diary*.

to be compared with monastery lists so that nothing would be lost to the King. From other abbeys come accounts of fires being made of the woodwork to melt down the lead stripped from the church roof. Bells were melted down for gun metal or sold to other churches. There is a long tradition that one Nuneaton bell still survives in Wolvey church.

The roofless church would soon fall into ruin. The rest of the monastic buildings suffered the fate of many other abbeys: grant to a new lay owner and conversion to his manor house. Nuneaton was granted to Sir Marmaduke Constable, whose family came from Flamborough in Yorkshire. Marmaduke's father, Sir Robert Constable, had been one of the leaders of the unsuccessful northern rebellion in 1536 known as the Pilgrimage of Grace, and had been executed the following year. Why the King should grant Nuneaton to a rebel's son is not at all clear. One clue, however, hints at a possible reason. The endorsement on the 1539 surrender deed bears Marmaduke's name. He had possibly proved his loyalty by joining Cromwell's commissioners and was now getting his reward. The situation is further confused by a 1539 priory lease to Ralph Sadler, Gentleman of the Chamber and royal official, of the Habyte house in the precinct and its associated demesne lands for 99 years. The lease was confirmed in 1540 by the Court of Augmentations (set up to administer former monastic property) but reduced to 21 years. Shortly after, the grant, including the lands in Sadler's lease, was made to Sir Marmaduke. There is some slight evidence that Sadler was compensated for his lost lease.

Sir Marmaduke soon set about adapting the priory's domestic buildings to convert them into a comfortable manor house. Excavation has revealed an aumbrey (cupboard) cut into the south-east corner of the warming room and a new brick and tile hearth close by. The siting of this fireplace suggests that the large warming room was now divided into a number of smaller apartments. Documentary evidence

37 The priory or Bar Pool water mill, 1723. Henry Beighton produced this detailed drawing of the priory mill which stood behind Earls Road. The mill had an overshot wheel whereby water fell on to the top of the wheel, turning it by gravity. The Bar Pool was drained by 1771 when the Coventry Canal crossed its site.

for such changes comes in a contract between Constable and a local carpenter, Leonard Johnson. Johnson agreed to 'syle' (panel) the walls and ceilings, portals and doors of six rooms and the gallery on the cloister. The style throughout is to be 'antyke wurke', which probably indicates a return to classical ornament characteristic of the Renaissance period.

A more detailed description of Constable's manor house appears in an inventory of the buildings made in 1561. Marmaduke had died the previous year and his son Robert intended to lease the property to Mary Dymmocke, widow:

> *The Halle* First the Syling rownd aboute within the same, 2 wyndowes fully glaced, 2 portalls, 3 dores with Benches aggreing to the Syling, 3 great tables and 3 Formes besides the glass prised at
>
> £26 13s. 4d.

The buttree and Sellar An Aumbrey, a close byend, one great Boorde before the wyndowe, an old Arke, 2 shelvys, 3 pannes to laze barrells upon, 2 Barrells for beare, a fourme, An Ark with a cover, 3 short Boardes or theales (besydes two wyndowes fully glased) prysed at
23s. 4d.

The Kytchyn and howses of office there A table on a frame, 2 sestarnes of leade, 5 boordes, 2 iron cheanes or potthangles, 5 shelves, an Aumbrey, A payre of mustard quernes, one doore lying upon tressills (wanting), a powdryng troughe with a cover, a great boorde before the ston wyndowes prised at
£7 10s. 8d.

The dynyng Chamber and four other chambers on that Roe One portall with 2 doores, 5 cupboordes and tenne wyndowes fully glased beside the glasse prised at
£3 12s. 8d.

The steare head in to the dynyng chamber Three wyndoes fully glased

The little Studdye One windowe fully glased and the studdy syled close with boxes, benches and lockes besides
£3

The 2 galeries 4 wyndowes glased and one cupboord besides the glasse prised at
20d. vacat

The chambers over and nere the gates 2 payre of playn bedstedes prised at
2s.

4 wyndowes glased unprised

The brewhouse and howses of office there 2 great brewing leades a little Sesterne of lead without the brewhouse parcel of the condyt, 2 mashe fattes, 2 yelyng fattes, a keelar, a kneading troughe, a pipe of leade servyng the great leades, a great Sesterne of lead to steepe In and a mowlding table prised at
£31 13s. 4d.

The grene chambers and other on that syde The Syling round about within the same, one Cupboord, 2 square Boordes, 4 joynd fourmes, 1 cheare, 3 Bedsteddes, 6 wyndowes fully glased besydes the glass prised at
£7 16s. 8d.

60 couple of black conyes and 60 couple of store carpes after there tale

Item Forty doores and 23 lockes within the said manor house.

[British Library Add. Ch. 48871]

The Tudor Town and its Inhabitants

Within three years of becoming lord of Nuneaton, Sir Marmaduke Constable began a detailed inquiry concerning his new possessions. All freeholders and the various types of tenant were summoned to the manor court hall to provide details of their land holdings: tenure, location, annual value, rent and other relevant information. Their answers were recorded in Latin by the clerk to provide a nearly complete survey of Nuneaton manor as it was on 10 October 1543. For easier reference, a brief summary in English of each holding was produced in 1544. The whole rental is a unique document for the town. By reconstructing plot boundaries, many of which survived up to modern redevelopment, it has been possible to map the town as it was in 1543.

The street plan of Tudor Nuneaton is substantially that of the modern town centre. Constable's Rental describes 169 occupied properties in Nuneaton town. Church End and Bond End together had 38 houses and there were a further 41 around the Market Place, Bridge Street and Bakehouse Lane (now Newdegate Street). Most heavily populated was the Abbey End with 75 houses, plus 11 more properties, including Constable's manor house, within the former priory walls. Only two houses are listed for Coton or Wash End (Queen's Road), low-lying with Wash Brook running down its middle and the south side in Coton parish. The two remaining houses were at Swans Yeat and Wykey End (both Croft Road).

Just over half the properties were owned by freeholders. Of the rest, 14 were held on some form of long lease and the remainder rented by the year. The 169 occupied houses, with the vicarage and six cottages on church land, would yield a total population for Nuneaton town of some 800 inhabitants.

By using Constable's Rental together with other contemporary documents, it is possible to reconstruct a Tudor 'town trail'; to walk with informed imagination through its streets and see its buildings much as they were in the mid-16th century.

St Nicolas Church stood on its slight eminence at the south end of Church Street, looking across Cawdell Holmes—four large enclosed crofts—to the River Anker. The vicarage stood north-east of the church, the forerunner of the later building. The probate inventory of George Downes, vicar of Nuneaton who died in 1583, lists seven rooms: hall, parlour, study, kitchen and buttery with chambers over the parlour and study. The vicarage was of average size and typical of local houses at that time. In the angle between Church End and the Vicarage or Back Lane was a croft belonging to the church with six cottages fronting the main street and the parish tithe barn behind them. North of these cottages, Church End was built up on both sides, the house plots still extending to the river and Back Lane (Vicarage Street) respectively. One house is of especial interest. William Everatt had 'one pece of ground … called a wayndowe and payth yerely at the said feast one capon'. The Latin survey adds that the land was for extending his hall on to the highway and was granted to William's uncle, John Everatt, by Agnes Olton, prioress, in 1523. The property eventually became the *King's Head* public house (a 17th-century building now demolished), which retained the large bay window projecting on to the pavement. The successors of William Everatt continued to use his window space well into the mid-20th century.

As Church End became Bond End so the character of the buildings changed. Here stood several of the traditional peasant farms whose medieval tenants had been 'bound' to the manor. Typical is John Christopher's farm sited in the modern Bond Street near the railway

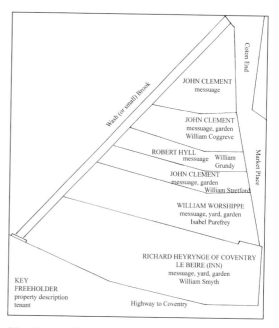

38 Market Place, south-west side in 1543. The Constable Rental of 1543 gives a detailed description of properties and boundaries in Nuneaton, thereby enabling a reconstruction of the town in that year.

station. He had 'one house covered in straw', i.e. thatched, comprising 'an hall, a kitchen, a chamber, a celler and other necessarie howses'. There was also 'one barn newly builded covered with tyles' and other barns, stables and farm buildings. The whole site including a yard and backside covered one acre. John Christopher had three crofts close to his farm house and 2½ yardlands totalling 40 acres in the open fields.

Bridge Street, only half the width of the modern road and lined with houses, gardens and even orchards, linked Church End to the Market Place. Mill Lane led from the south side of Bridge Street to Richard Checkley's three town mills—two water- and one horse-powered—standing on the site used for grinding corn from before Domesday right up to 1976. The mill pools were close to the present George Eliot Gardens.

The plan of the Market Place will be perfectly familiar to people today. The medieval open square now had a central island of permanent buildings with the shambles or meat market at its east end. Facing Coventry Street was the town cross surrounded by eight stone pillars supporting an octagonal cross chamber capped by the market bell, always rung to signal the start of trading. The cross was demolished in 1810 but contemporary sketches show what it was like. Offenders could be placed in the pillory which stood at the west end of the market. A further public punishment may have been a ducking stool since the old way across the river (between Bridge Street and Bakehouse Lane) was called Cukstole Lane.

By this time Nuneaton could boast three inns around the Market Place. The *Bear* stood on the Coventry Street corner, while the *Ram* in the recently built market centre block was close to the site of the later *Board Inn*. The

39 The *King's Head* (left) in Church Street is a 17th-century public house. Its prominent bay window, first granted to the Everatt family by the priory in 1523, survived until 1960.

principal inn, the *Crown*, was situated on the old north-west side. This building survived much altered until 1913, having been called the *Old Crown*, the *Bull* and finally the *Newdegate Arms*. Constable's tenant (and later owner) Richard Ratclyffe also rented three chambers above the Moot or Manor Court Hall, which stood just in front of his inn. At some later time the Moot Hall became part of the *Crown*. Early photographs show the projecting section in Newdegate Square, a traffic hazard even in Edwardian Nuneaton! The 1607 probate inventory for a later Richard Ratclyffe describes the *Crown Inn* and its contents in great detail. It had the usual rooms: hall, parlour, green parlour, buttery and kitchen, with various specialised rooms around a courtyard with the street gates. There was probably a second yard containing mainly stables and barns with a gatehouse. The *Crown* had at least ten chambers, some situated over the stables. Outside was the 'sign of the crowne', while on the parlour wall hung 'a table of the armes of England'.

Abbey End was closely lined on both sides with cottages up to the priory precinct wall near Cole (now Abbey) Green. Many of the original burgage plots had been sub-divided lengthways into half burgages of some 25 feet frontage. This allowed for more houses without extending the built-up area, a practice which was to create great problems by the mid-19th century. Nuneaton does not seem to be under population pressure in the 1540s. Indeed, there is evidence of under-development. Five Abbey End properties are described as crofts and may never have been built on. Several others are called tofts, indicating that they had formerly been house plots. William Worshippe had orchards on the site of three cottages and Robert Fyndern's heirs owned the site of two more.

Two further blocks of property had been demolished for industrial use. Roger Mantil, tanner, occupied the site of three cottages and a former tenement, presumably for his tanyard, while James A. Lee Walker (i.e. cloth fuller) had

40 Market Place and the *Peacock Inn*. This was a small building with twin gables which probably dates from the late-Tudor period, though it was not an inn until much later. It was replaced by a new public house by 1914.

41 The *Old Newdegate Arms* Yard, *c.*1904. This inn appears in the Constable Rental as the *Crown*. It was later known as the *Old Crown*, the *Bull* and finally the *Newdegate Arms*, following its acquisition by the Arbury family. The overhanging building suggests Tudor origins.

two cottages and a waste half-burgage called the Tenter Yard. This was where woollen cloth, having been cleansed and felted in a fulling or walk mill, was stretched on tenter-hooks. The 1543 Rental has Walkmyll Close on the north side of Wash Lane, while Pool Bank Street recalls the head of water, raised by damming the Wash Brook, needed to drive the fulling mill. All traces of a pool would have been swept away when the later gasworks was built on the same site.

Beyond the westernmost houses in Abbey End lay the late priory precinct, increasingly known as Manor Court. The Constable rental in fact describes two courts. The inner court comprised the former nuns' buildings, now the manor house, while the outer court covered the remainder of the 34-acre area. Here the principal building was the Habyte: the abbot's or prior's house. To its south stood the house next to the Habyte and Fyndern's House, William Fyndern being the last Receiver of the priory. Along the way to the gatehouse lay three more tenements and the priory mill stood below the Barpool dam.

The triangle between present-day Abbey Street, Queen's Road and Manor Court Road was largely filled by Countess Close, a 20-acre pasture, and Walkmyll Close. South of the outer court was Countess Wood and then enclosed fields stretching towards Stockingford. The Outwoods and Johnswood covered the western end of Camphill, with a further wood, the Great Ley, occupying the modern quarry area down to the boundary with Weddington and Caldecote.

An insight into the lives of the inhabitants can be gained from the 'pains' or penalties issued by the manor court between 1570 and 1572. One abiding concern was the state of the town. Regulations were made concerning cleaning of streets and of the ditches which drained the town into the river:

> A payne made than no person shall sweepe downe any muck in the stretes to th'annoyance of his neighbour but shall carye it away in payne of every defalte   4d.

> A payne sett that the Tenantes of the Cownteise Close do skower their dyches from the Cowntesse Woodde Corner downeward till they come to William Wright his yardes end And also William Wright, Alexander Turnor and John Suffock shall lykewise skower their dyches in pene to everye offendor   3s. 4d.

Another pain tackled the problem of wagons blocking the often narrow streets. This must be Nuneaton's earliest parking regulation:

> A payne laide that all th'inhabytauntes dwelling betwene the Towne bridge and William Ambrose and betwene Johan Hobbys and John Lawrenne and lykewyse throughout the wholle towne shall not sett eyther waynes nor cartes in the streetes nor laye any [mounting] block without his house easinge in payne of every defalte   3s. 4d.

Properties were often a source of neighbourly friction and house-holders were encroaching on the highway by adding lean-to buildings (pentyses) to the front of their houses:

> A payne sett that John Oughton sett his house upright that it do not Anoye his neighbour Richarde Vynsent Before mydsomer in payne of   20d.

> A Payne that Thomas Rydley and Randell Webb do agree with the lord for the penteyses that they have made between this and the next leete or ells do cawse the same to be taken downe agayne before the seid leete in payne of   10s.

The last major concern of the court was the regulation of tradesmen, especially in furthering the prosperity of the market and local crafts. The two following pains were to build up market trade and to ensure raw materials for the tanners:

> A Payne sett that all that dwell within the towne and paryshe of Eton that hathe wares to sell that every of them doe Furnyshe their owne markett in payne for every defalt so taken or knowen   12d.

> A payne layde that all the Buchers within the towne of Eton and also all the owtbuchers that come to the markett shall not sell any beiffe mutton nor lambe excepte he or they do bringe the hide or skyn into the markett in payne of every defalte   3s. 4d.

42 Market Place: Deacon & Son, saddler's. Deacon's certainly believed in putting their wares on show. Leather working was one of the important trades in the Tudor-Stuart period. The shop was demolished when the post office was built on this site in 1912.

Occasionally a pain will give unexpected information. It is interesting to find what was sold in the market; to learn that trades stood in specific places is a bonus:

> A pain leid that all Tanners, shoomakers, glovers, bakers, Chaundlers and Smythes with their iron ware shall everye markett day hereafter kepe theyr stalls with suche ware as they have presentlye to sell, the bakers and chaundlers to stand in theyr accustomed place ... in payne of 3s. 4d. for eny defawte and for the better execucion of this payne it is ordeyned that the Balyf of Nuneyton and the Constable shall take view every markett daye who maketh defawlte and present the same at the next leet.
>
> [British Library Add. Roll 49700]

For Nuneaton town with its 800 or so inhabitants, the manor court of freeholders and manorial officials was an efficient form of local government. It was well able to deal with the everyday problems of the small community.

King Edward VI Grammar School
The foundation of the earliest school in Nuneaton came about in a quite unexpected way. In 1507 John Leke of Nuneaton gave to St Nicolas' Church a house 'between the high-way [Church End] and the mill pond' which he had bought some fifteen years earlier. This gift was to endow a chantry priest to say mass for the souls of the Leke family. John Leke's will, dated 2 June 1508, included the following:

> Also I will that all the lands, tenements etc. in Nuneaton which are in the hands of my feofees for this purpose with other lands to be acquired by Richard Astell to the value of 4 marks [53s. 4d.] shall maintain a chaplain in the parish church of St. Nicolas for ever, to pray for my parents and for those to whom my father was in any way bound in satisfaction, and for their Obits to be yearly done at Nuneaton and Erdebury if they can be enjoyed without interruption by the king. Otherwise I will that they be sold and distributed to the poor in works of charity.

This final clause was to prove all-important. When John Leke made his will, it was most unlikely that the king, a fervent Catholic, would ever stop masses for departed souls. Following the break with Rome and the dissolution of all monastic houses the trustees of the chantry, realising the threat in the early 1540s, agreed to use the endowment for charity as the will allowed. They decided that a free school would meet John Leke's intentions and set about its foundation.

Their foresight paid off. Acts of 1545 and 1547 did lead to the closure of chantries. In 1548 the commissioner who visited this district had to report:

> Aboute syxe yeres paste yt was concluded amongst the parochians theare by the consent of the heyres of the same Leke that the Revenues thereof with more gyven of theyr Devocion shoolde be convertyd to the mayntenaunce of a scoolmaster theare, the which for that yt hathe not been convertyd to the use of A Chauntry within these syxe yeres I take it to be owte of the Compas of the Statute, and therefore I have omitted the certificate thereof.

Thus the charity funds escaped confiscation and the school survived. The endowment, however, proved insufficient, so some two years later a petition was sent to King Edward VI asking for a royal charter for a Free Grammar School in his name and for a grant of more property. Lands of the dissolved Guilds of Holy Trinity and Corpus Christi in Coventry were granted to the school together with a Charter and Common Seal. Nuneaton's King Edward VI

Grammar School legally came into being on 11 May 1552.

The school had 12 governors with Sir Marmaduke Constable as first chairman. They were to appoint a schoolmaster learned in the Latin tongue, subject to confirmation by the Bishop of Coventry and Lichfield, at a salary of £10 a year. This fixed salary was to cause much trouble during the school's first hundred years since, by the 1580s, the income from endowments had nearly doubled. Headmasters, including Richard Inge before 1615 and his successor Anthony Reay, claimed a greater share of the income and freedom from control by the governors. The controversy led to expensive litigation ending in victory for the headmaster.

The governors had certainly used much of their revenue to build a new school house. The location of the earliest school is unknown; possibly in the former Leke chapel or in the house near the mill pond. In 1595 the governors bought a decayed messuage which stood on the north side of the churchyard. The building accounts still survive and show the work took some four years to complete. To strengthen their legal position, the governors finally produced a set of Orders which show how

43   King Edward VI Grammar School. The old Grammar School in St Nicolas church-yard dates from 1595-9. It was rebuilt in 1696 and served as the school until 1880. Badly damaged in the 1941 air raid, it was later sympathetically restored as the parish office.

they intended the school to be run. They include:

> That the schoolmaster lovinglie shall receive all manner of schollars and teach them freelie to his best power ... That all the Schollers if they be not far from the school be there present in Summer at six of the clock and in Winter at seven, and when they be gathered and assembled the schoolmaster shall use praier every morning beinge schools daie before he begin to teach that day. And when they shall depart from the school shall use praier in like sorts ... we will that our Schoolmaster dilligentlie see that his schollars come to school ornately and cleanely in such apparel as they have. And that they use noe leud or corrupt conversation ...

The latent tension exploded once more during the Commonwealth period. Royalist headmaster William Barford had been appointed in the reign of Charles I. Fearing he might lose his post, he gave the headship to William Trevis in exchange for a £10 annuity. This exchange, approved by the governors in 1655, was to prove a source of great trouble. Trevis was also a staunch Royalist, who had been ejected from his fellowship at Trinity College Cambridge for supporting the monarchy. Nuneaton, like neighbouring Coventry, was largely Parliamentarian in sympathy. The vicar Richard Pyke, appointed by Oliver Cromwell in 1655, had managed to keep his living at the restoration of Charles II in 1660. A political and religious dimension had been added to the century-old friction between governors and headmaster.

Trouble started in 1662 when one of the governors, Mr Ralph Wright, incited the scholars to rebel against William Trevis. But more serious was the second outbreak in 1665. On 28 November the scholars, who had been armed by some of the townspeople, refused the head entry to the school. The following morning Mr Trevis, according to his own account, was greeted by 'the discharge of pistolls and guns'. He almost persuaded the scholars to surrender but the parish clerk, Luke Mortimer,

44 King Edward VI Grammar School. During post-war restoration, several roof beams were uncovered on which were carved the date of building 1596 and the initials of Edward Povey, Semore Mantill and bailiffs John Suffolk and Robert Hill. Nicholas Lynney, carpenter, was in charge of the building project.

urged them not to give in, 'falsely alleadging that I had brought two Bindles of birch to punish them with'.

On Thursday 30 November matters became even more serious. William Smyth, tanner, and Ralph Wright, nephew of the 1662 governor, went into the school armed with a great gun and a pistol: 'They conducted the schollers out and twice or thrice att midnight shott off their guns and pistolls against my dwelling house, incourageing the schollers to doe the like, broke my windores in severall places.' The following day Mr Trevis finally decided to bring in the civil powers, and informed Mr Serjant Newdigate of Arbury, who rode into town that evening. Approaching the school, Richard Newdigate 'was most ungratefully requited by the discharge of a pistoll

45 Nuneaton Vicarage. Replacing an earlier seven-roomed vicarage, this imposing building was erected by Richard Pyke, vicar 1655-78, and appears in the Hearth Tax returns for 1662. The attractive building with its Flemish gables was enlarged by Robert Savage after 1845. When a new vicarage was built in 1974, the old one fortunately survived as commercial premises.

in his face'. This attack on lawful authority frightened the scholars, who quickly fled through the back window and over the vicarage garden leaving the school in disorder: 'Heer lying bread and beef and turnepp there spoons heer an old blanket, in one place a sword, in another a pistoll, in a third a Pitcher stood full of Ale, the windores broken, the boards and wainscott of the seates torn up for fuel.'

On 9 December events took a bizarre turn. Following the vicar's orders, Luke Mortimer as town crier rang his bell during the Saturday market and proclaimed:

> Bee it known … that, My Master, Mr. Richard Pyke … doth from his soule, hate, abhorr abominate and detest whatsoever Mr. Trevis falsly and untruly alleadged and declared against him yesterday in Caldecott Hall.
> [Warwick CR 136 C 13 680.]

The previous day some of the rioters had been examined by Justice Purefoy at Caldecote, with Smyth and Mortimer being bound over to the Assizes. Returning to the town they had concocted the story that the head had implicated the vicar.

With the civil authorities involved, the governors were in a weak position. They only totalled six, so Gervase Buswell, as chairman, chose six supporters to complete the required number. The following year they took legal action to dismiss the headmaster. Their indictment included the following charges:

> That his cruel and hard usage of the Schollars hath driven almost all the schollars away insomuch that they are fallen from 100 to 20 and scarce so many. That he seldom or never comes to Church with his Scholars as the order directeth, and that his Schollars are given to horrible cursing and swearing …
> That he hath severall times debauched himself with excessive drinking and neglects his school, by frequenting of Bowling Alleys … and chargeth his schollars to play in the school when he is absent so that the townsmen may not see them.

When the bishop and an Assize judge heard the case, Trevis was the victor. He survived another case in 1680 when it was decided that he should keep the school rents of £80 but pay an usher £20 to teach, an undertaking that he delayed for another ten years. Trevis remained head till 1698. By 1696 the school had been rebuilt and still remains as the parish church office, having survived extensive air-raid damage in 1941.

Five

EXPLOITING THE LAND:
EARLY MODERN AGRICULTURE AND INDUSTRY

Throughout the 16th century local farmers tilled their open-field strips as they had done for nearly a thousand years. But continuity can prove deceptive. The old open-field system was constantly being modified to meet changing economic and social conditions.

The standard holding was still the traditional peasant yardland of some 25 acres, but by 1543 these holdings had become concentrated into fewer hands. William Everatt had five and a quarter yardlands and William Astell three. Sir Anthony Coke had leased the former Arbury Priory two and a half yardlands to the bailiff Edward Povey, and John Christopher and Thomas Broke each farmed two yardlands. The 14 demesne yardlands at Horeston were farmed jointly by John Watts and Richard and Robert Vynson. Both John Watts and Robert Vynson rented additional holdings from the lord or from other tenants. Though four men worked less than two yardlands each, the trend was towards larger, capitalist, rather than small-scale, subsistence, farming.

The trend was to bring new land into productive use. There are several leases from the Constable period in which tenants agreed to clear woodland for pasture. Most of them refer to parts of the Great Lee Wood from Tuttle Hill to Weddington and Caldecote and to the modern Camp Hill area. By 1655 Great Horeston Wood between Horeston Fields and Attleborough was also converting to pasture. The task was immense and protracted. Between 1690 and 1692 wheelwright Joseph Nutt bought 140 oak trees from Horeston for £1,015. More pasture was needed for cheese production. Warwickshire cheese was exported as far as London and most 17th-century Nuneaton farmers had large quantities stored in their upper chambers. They were obviously aware of, and responsive to, market forces.

Market awareness was not new. The late 15th century had seen a rising demand for wool which was met—with disastrous results. Early Tudor landlords, realising that sheep would bring greater profit than customary farm rents, turned out peasant farmers and created vast sheep-runs. Two local villages suffered this fate. In 1491 Thomas, Marquis of Dorset, evicted ten families from his manor of Weddington and enclosed 300 acres of arable. Sixty people were 'driven into idleness' and Weddington became virtually a deserted village. Stretton Baskerville suffered a similar fate. Thomas Twyford had destroyed seven dwellings to enclose 160 acres in 1489. He then sold the manor to Henry Smith who completed the process. The *Domesday of Enclosures* (1517-18) tells the sad story:

> There were twelve houses each with a garden and close and four other cottages [in 1494]. There were 640 acres under the plough as far back as human memory went. Smith built ditches and banks to enclose the fields and make his sheep-run. He wilfully allowed the houses to fall into ruin and turned the fields

from cultivation to be a feeding place for brute animals. Eighty people who worked here went away sorrowfully to idleness; to drag out a miserable life, and truthfully—so to die in misery.

Stretton Baskerville was never re-occupied but Weddington reverted to arable farming in the 17th century and developed as a 20th-century suburb for Nuneaton.

The lands west of the river, including the former priory demesne and the part of Stockingford in Nuneaton manor, had never been open-field strips. Once cleared from the forest, they were farmed as small enclosed fields. The separate Stockingford manor, which extended from Whittleford through Galley Common to Ansley, again, had been taken in from the ancient Forest of Arden. It had no nucleated village centre, just a scattering of isolated farms surrounded by enclosed fields. The area today still retains some of this old landscape.

Though change did occur, much remained traditional. The manor court still made communal decisions about farming practice. It fixed the date when animals must be driven off the stubble before ploughing: 'There is a payne layde that all men shall keepe their Cattell from the Corne after the Feast of all Sowles next in payne for every beast so taken 4d. and for every flock shepe lykwise 12d.' Meadows were still allocated yearly by lot and the portions staked out: 'A payne that all the husbandmen shall meete upon the Marke Daye to stake their medowes in pene to any one making defalt 12d.' Disputes were still settled by the Jury, which represented the common memory of manorial practice: 'A payne is sett that all the Jury shall mete together on mydsommer eve with all the husbandmen By seven of the Clock in the mornynge to refourme things that Be Amysse in the Feelde on payne to every man that is awaye without especyall cause to forfeyte

46 Weddington: deserted village site 1990. Until the 20th century Weddington church had stood almost isolated in the fields. The original village, depopulated in 1491, probably lay between the church and the river. Enclosure for sheep grazing 'fossilised' the former open-field strips, here clearly visible behind the church.

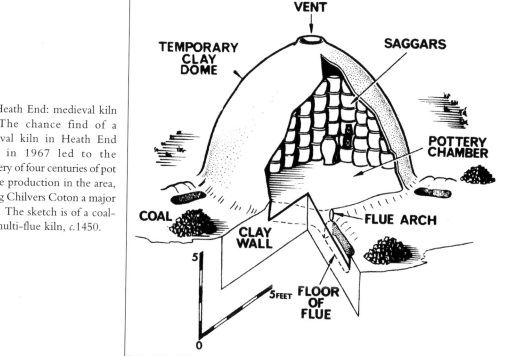

47 Heath End: medieval kiln site. The chance find of a medieval kiln in Heath End Road in 1967 led to the discovery of four centuries of pot and tile production in the area, making Chilvers Coton a major centre. The sketch is of a coal-fired multi-flue kiln, c.1450.

and lose 20s.' However, the process of change from agriculture to industry was already evident. Local medieval industry was mainly a by-product of farming. Walkmill Close and the Tenter Yard have already been mentioned as evidence for a woollen industry, while woodland clearance provided raw material for several wheelwrights. Tanning, too, flourished during these two centuries, together with shoemaking and general leather work.

Extractive industries also have a long history. The earliest known pottery made in this area came from Romano-British kilns at Hartshill and Griff. In 1967 the chance find of medieval kilns in the Heath End and Bermuda area led to large-scale excavation. The result was the discovery that Chilvers Coton was a major pottery and tile production centre from around 1250 up to the 17th century. John Butterton's tile house on Bar Green below Tuttle Hill was making bricks and tiles in 1543 and there are several references to brickmakers in 17th-century documents.

Coal extraction also has early origins though these are difficult to date. The Templars' Coton manor accounts for 1309 mention the sale of 'sea coal', and mining in Nuneaton dates from at least 1338, when a dispute is recorded between John le Colyere and Richard le Synkere. The coal was extracted from the outcrop of the seams by shallow bell-pits. Easily won coal led to accusations of illegal mining at the priory manor court. In 1350 the prioress complained that Richard Gibbes and others had with armed force dug in the private land of the priory and carried away sea coal to the value of £40. Three years later the prioress again complained that John de Allesworth had dug in her ground at Nuneaton, taking marsh coal to the value of 10s. Another mining offence was failing to fill in worked-out pits. In 1343 William Wagestaffe was ordered on pain of a 2s. fine to fill up the coal pit which he had opened at Stockingford.

The best example of early mining practice comes from a lease made in 1583 by Margaret

48   Bell Pits, 1911. Early mining left little evidence above ground apart from crater-like depressions on the surface. Striking miners in the 20th century dug coal from the abandoned outcrop areas using medieval techniques for sinking shallow bell-shaped pits. This photograph must date from the 1911 strike and have been taken in the Stockingford area.

Knollys, lady of the manor, to Edward Crosland, Robert Rotchell, Edward Matha and William Shawe, colliers, of Nuneaton. The lessees could dig coal in Blackwater Field (from which Blackatree Road gets its name) for three years, paying £6 13s. 4d. and 'six wayne loades of good great Coles' yearly. For the period of the lease Mrs Knollys promised not to let any other coal mines in the Great Stocking, thus giving the four miners a practical monopoly. They in turn agreed that:

They shall orderly and workmanly take the coles before theym to the bottom in every pitt … and shall also fill upp or cause to be filled upp with yearthe and slecke all and evey sinke, pitt and pittes … and further there shall not be in the work at any tyme above six men to gett coles.

[British Library Add. Ch. 49848]

These three clauses show how small-scale mining was. The miners had to extract all the coal in each pit and fill up the hole. The lease refers to pits in the plural assuming that several will be worked during the quite short three-year lease. The limit of six 'face-workers' emphasises how small the pits were. The three main seams out-cropped at a short distance from each other. The usual practice was to open a series of bell-pits along each seam. Once the coal was extracted from the shallowest level, new lines would be opened into the deeper seams.

Associated with the coal measures was ironstone. A 1551 lease of the priory mill refers to bloomsmiths working along the Barpool Brook. This old way of working involved heating the ironstone to a paste and beating with hammers to remove impurities and produce a bloom of wrought iron. By 1540 the newer blast furnace had just come into use in the Weald of Kent. The blast raised the temperature sufficiently to burn out the impurities and produce six to ten times more iron than the bloomery hearth did. In 1547 the new blast furnace was introduced to Nuneaton. Sir Marmaduke Constable agreed a lease for ten years with James Heyley of Myryvall (Merevale) and his brother William of Handsworth. Sir Marmaduke was to set up:

> Of his owne costes and charges and expenses within the lordshipe of Eton in the County of Warwick upon the ryver there called the water of Ankar one iron smithie, two blowe harthes and one brenne harthe with all maner of tooles and instrumentes necessarye for an iron smythie and also one payre of sybstantial floudgates necessarye for the same.
>
> [British Library Add. Ch. 48796]

The brenne or burning hearth was to break up the ironstone which was then loaded into the blow hearths or blast furnaces. The floodgates were to dam the river, providing a head of water for the wheel powering the bellows.

49   Tuttle Hill windmill. Early windmills have been located south of Hinckley Road, Hill Top and, improbably, next to the water mill at the lowest point of the town centre. The Tuttle Hill windmill dates from the 18th century though frequently it was rebuilt. Its unusual five sails were finally taken down in 1936.

50 Nuneaton Colliery Stables. Horse transport was the only means of moving coal before the coming of the canals and, later, railways. Horses remained the usual way of serving the local market well into the 20th century.

The Heyley brothers agreed to make at least eight blows of iron weekly, paying 2s. 6d. per blow; a minimum income for the lord of £1 a week. Sir Marmaduke augmented this income by selling to the iron workers charcoal from 'his wodes callyd the oute woodes' and ironstone from 'the pytt in Blacke water feld ready dygged'.

The approximate site of the ironworks can be established from the lease. The cartloads of charcoal would come down Tuttle Hill while the ironstone came along Vernons Lane; both routes leading to Abbey Green. The nearest way to the river was the track which still leads from Aston Road towards Weddington. The lease allowed carts to cross New Mill Field, east of the railway, and the Priest's Bridge. This bridge must have crossed the river upstream of the Change Brook, which formed the manor boundary. The ironworks, then, lay close to Weddington Road between the Change Brook and the later Midland Railway bridge.

It is not known if the ironworks proved successful since it does not appear in later rentals. Even so, its establishment here in 1547 put Nuneaton at the forefront as Britain entered a new age of technology.

Six

SEVENTEENTH-CENTURY NUNEATON SOCIETY

Although St Nicolas parish registers start in 1588, gaps limit their usefulness until 1653 onwards, when they are generally complete and can yield vital information about population patterns by counting baptisms and burials. The 70-year period 1671-1740 records 4,504 baptisms and 3,891 burials. To provide a base figure, the 415 households in the 1670 Hearth Tax return have been multiplied by 4½. This puts the population of Nuneaton parish, including Attleborough and Stockingford, at 1,867 in 1670—nearly double that estimated for 1543. The surplus 613 baptisms would take the population total to 2,480 by 1740, a rise of one-third in 70 years. The total does not allow for migration, but this was unlikely to be a major factor when industrial change was slow and limited.

Over the period, the surplus of baptisms over burials averages only nine per year. The precarious balance was seriously upset by a wave of epidemics which ravaged North Warwickshire between 1728 and 1730. The five-year period 1726-30 has 198 more burials than baptisms. Rising birth and falling death rates led to recovery within ten years.

51 Abbey Gate corner. This 17th-century timber-framed house gives a good idea of the architecture of the Stuart town. In 1898 it made way for Reginald Stanley's *Gate Hotel*; an act of Victorian vandalism which, paradoxically, gave the modern town centre its most striking building.

This slow, uncertain growth is highlighted when the demographic history of late-17th-century families is examined through reconstitution techniques by which families are 're-assembled' from register entries. For the period 1661-1700, 371 families have been reconstituted giving a sound base for statistics. The median or mid-point of each range of statistics shows how various factors worked together to limit the population increase.

The median marriage age was 25 years for men and 25 years 2 months for women. This is quite late and obviously reduces the child-bearing period for wives. The first child was born within a year of marriage but later conceptions were well spaced out, probably by extended lactation, with the interval rising to 29 months. Most marriages were of short duration—the average age at death was just over 48 years—and the typical number of children per marriage was five. Not unexpectedly, children also died early. In fact, a third of all children died before the age of 21. The critical period was infancy: of children buried, 43.1 per cent were below a year old; 72.9 per cent were under five. This reduces the figure for surviving children to about three per marriage, sufficient to maintain the population but with little surplus. Death was an ever-present fact in 17th-century Nuneaton.

52 Abbey Street. Somehow this solitary timber-framed house survived Victorian rebuilding and the general dereliction of post-war Abbey Street. It could not escape the planners and disappeared under Lexington Court council flats.

From tax returns it is possible to discern varying levels in local society according to wealth. When Charles II regained his throne in 1660 the treasury was almost empty, so the government appealed to loyal subjects to contribute to a Free Gift to the king in 1661. Nuneaton's response was muted, with donations from about a third of householders. Amounts varied from Rev. Richard Pyke's £5 down to one shilling. The vicar's generosity can possibly be explained by his need, as a Cromwellian appointment, to hold on to his benefice. His loyal example was scarcely followed by his parishioners. Some 85 per cent of the contributors gave less than five shillings.

In 1662 the Free Gift was replaced by the Hearth Tax. This imposed a charge on tenants of two shillings annually for each fireplace. It was intended as a wealth tax, the occupiers of the largest houses paying most. Those who were too poor to pay church and poor rates, and whose property was valued at less than £1, were exempted. The proportion of the exempt poor remained fairly constant between 1663 and 1674, varying from 45 per cent to 53 per cent of households.

Social difference is also apparent in occupational groups extracted from documents between 1651-1700. Occupations have been traced for 387 inhabitants during this fifty-year period. Traders and craftsmen with 49 per cent make the largest group, followed by farmers at 33 per cent, and gentry and professions at a mere six per cent. The poor are rarely documented and, at three per cent for servants and nine per cent for labourers and miners, are vastly under-represented. But the general pattern is quite clear: Nuneaton had a small gentry class above a much larger group of traders, craftsmen and farmers employing an untold legion of wage labourers of little substance.

The employing classes also feature strongly in surviving probate inventories. These had to be made when the personal wealth and possessions, but not land, of the deceased might

53 Abbey Green: the old *Plough and Ball*. This thatched public house—in itself a local rarity—seems a typical brick-built cottage, but its barely visible stone plinth suggests timber framing under a later brick skin. In the Edwardian period a new, larger *Plough and Ball* replaced the old one and still survives as *Town Talk*.

be in excess of £5. There are 144 Nuneaton probate inventories for the period at Lichfield Record Office. Again, the poorer rarely appear. The gross value of the inventories runs from Thomas Veasey's £2 5s. 2d. upwards. For the less wealthy the upper limit seems to be £70, and some two-thirds of the inventories are in this group. The top third falls mainly between £100 and £373, with Job Muston's £505, William Woodford's £522 and John Lee's £563 standing apart from the rest. There is a reasonable correlation between wealth and status. As might be expected, the highest average value at £187 belonged to the three men of gentry status. Traders and craftsmen averaged out at £95, with farmers at £89. The few labourers with possessions totalling between £4 and £53 had a £24 average.

Personal wealth was largely tied to occupation. Over half the total amount was tied up in farm or trade stock, while only a fifth came from household possessions. This is completely opposite to modern experience where personal wealth is mostly reflected in our possessions and savings. Cash made up a mere seven per cent, but a further 15 per cent of the total wealth consisted of debts due to the estate. Some of this represents goods and produce sold and awaiting payment, but the rest must be money lent out at interest, increasing the availability of capital in the area.

The inventories also provide information about farming practice. From counting farm stock, it appears that the average Nuneaton farmer had eight cattle, 30 sheep, three or four horses and a pig. This was definitely small-scale but, again, there were larger farmers emerging. Five inventories had 21-50 cattle and five over 100 sheep. Crops are harder to evaluate because amounts or acreage were rarely recorded. Corn, mainly wheat and barley, was the main crop, with 99 mentions. Fodder for farming and transport was essential so 75 inventories record hay and 21 oats. The other staple food crop was peas, mentioned 36 times. One important farm product was cheese, with 46 mentions by number, weight or value (consistently £1 per hundredweight). With some farmers having up to 8 cwt and others between 36 and 128 cheeses, the amounts were obviously in excess of family needs and even local demand. Warwickshire cheese was celebrated and exported over great distances. In 1682 the Justices at Warwick Quarter Sessions complained of exploitation by London cheese factors and banned them for one year from trading within the county. The centre for the cheese trade was Atherstone which Defoe noted in the mid-1720s was: 'A town famous for a great cheese fair on the 8th of September from whence the great cheese factors carry the vast quantities they buy to Sturbridge fair … and here tis sold for the supply of the counties of Essex, Suffolk and Norfolk.'

Probate inventories usually list possessions room by room, thus unwittingly providing descriptions of the houses in which local people lived. The 126 inventories listed by rooms show houses which range from two rooms to the 17 of the newly rebuilt vicarage. The average size was six rooms: most frequently the hall, which was the living room, the more private parlour, and domestic offices such as a kitchen and buttery. The upper storey usually had chambers over the hall and parlour. Chambers tended to be used for storage; the best bedstead was most likely to be found in the parlour.

Though the houses of the more wealthy Nuneaton people were more than adequately furnished, the emphasis was on utility, not luxury. Ornaments and pictures rarely appear and there are only three time-pieces: Richard Pyke's gold watch, Richard Francis' clock and

Robert Hill's hour-glass. Books, usually just a Bible, appear in 22 inventories. Though Widow Dorothy Beale had 25 school books, the only real library was that of the vicar, Richard Pyke, whose 'whole Study of Books and other things there' was valued at £10.

One of the great achievements of the period was an increasingly efficient system of local government. Based on the parish, the existing nucleus of minister and churchwardens was augmented by surveyors of the highways in 1555 and overseers of the poor by 1601. Expenditure was met by rates on property and parishes were under the supervision of local magistrates who met four times yearly in Quarter Sessions. Most of Warwickshire's Quarter Sessions records for the 17th century have been published, giving a fascinating insight into many aspects of local life.

Rate collection—never popular—became an issue between Nuneaton town and its hamlets of Attleborough and Stockingford. This first emerges in 1628, when Nuneaton complained that the hamlets were refusing to pay their share. The matter was not finally settled until 1657:

> Upon information that divers of the inhabitants of Attelborowe have long been oppressed by unjust taxes, some great estates paying nothing and other poor people being hard taxed, it was prayed that an indifferent levy for the poor may be made by the pound rent upon all the lands and tenements in Attleborowe, they paying a third part against the town of Nuneaton.

Rate valuation was not the only financial problem. Parish officials sometimes found re-imbursement of expenses difficult to obtain. Parish constable Jonathan Lee died in 1661, during his year in office, £3 10s. 4d. out of pocket. It was January 1663 before his brother John obtained an order from Quarter Sessions for payment and costs. Two years later the overseers of the highways also complained that both they and the previous surveyors were owed money for work done.

Surveyors or overseers were chosen under the 1551 Highways Statute to maintain all

54 Chilvers Coton: Coventry Road. A substantial 17th-century house with an interesting Gothic window inserted. The house, on the George Eliot Street corner opposite Coton Infants School, was probably demolished in the late 1920s.

highways in the parish and levy rates for repairs. In 1626 the main task was to repair the bridge over the Anker on the way to Attleborough. The surveyors experienced not unfamiliar problems with the contractor:

> A taxation hath been made for the repair of Attleborowe bridge and composition was made with one Simondes that [he] for £20 should do all the workmanship and find carriage, which work he hath accordingly begun and almost finished, and if the rest be not done the cost already bestowed will be lost … It is now ordered that the said Simondes shall further set himself about the finishing of his work.

Eighteen months later the bridge was still uncompleted and 'beginneth to grow in decay again'. The court ordered parish constable William Loader to see the work finished.

The biggest burden laid on the parish officials was poor relief. The Elizabethan Poor Law Acts had made parishes responsible for those who could not survive without support. Relief only became available in the parish where the person was last legally settled, as defined in the 1662 Settlement Act. Parishes made every effort to keep relief costs low by removing paupers who could not prove legal settlement.

55 College Street: timber-frame construction. What seemed to be 19th-century brick cottages opposite the College for the Poor revealed this timber-frame wall on a rough stone plinth during demolition in the 1960s. Some panels retain the original wattle and daub infilling.

When parishes failed to agree, Quarter Sessions had to adjudicate. Their findings bring to light the sad stories of this usually submerged section of society. In 1655 the court heard:

> That Sarah, the wife of Richard Chamberlayne, with her two children (her husband being gone from her) did lately break into an house of Thomas Rose standing empty without a tenant in Arley, endeavouring to gain a settlement there, whereupon it was prayed that they might be removed to Non Eaton, the place of their last legal settlement … and the constable of Arley is to carry them away accordingly.

Those who were legally settled could expect help, however ungenerous, from their parish. When help was not forthcoming, the poor could always appeal to the Justices, as happened in 1642:

> Upon consideration of the petition of Christopher Glover of Stockenford in the parish of Nuneaton showing that he is a very poor man and hath five children and is lately stricken lame in his left arm and so in no way able to maintain himself and his children, it is ordered that the overseers of the poor shall place the three eldest children to be apprentices and that until they shall do so they shall pay 2s. weekly to the said Christopher Glover.

As well as paying relief, the overseers might have to shelter the homeless. This was the case, in 1660, with Thomas Arden of Nuneaton:

> Who hath long lived in the said town and is now grown very poor and aged and, for not paying his rent, is ejected out of his dwelling house and so destitute of lodging, the court doth order that the churchwardens, overseers of the poor and inhabitants of Nuneaton do provide and allow to Thomas Arden a convenient house for the habitation of himself, his wife and child.

Some misfortunes were beyond the scope of poor law provision. Insurance was virtually non-existent in the provinces so robbery or fire could spell ruin. Here the Justices could order a general collection throughout the county. One such unfortunate incident happened in the dwelling house of Henry Flood, carrier, of Nuneaton. On 14 March 1658 there broke out:

> A lamentable and fearful fire which speadily consumed and burnt to the ground the same with the most part of his household stuff and all of his barning and stabling, being in all about ten bays of building, together with his hay, fodder, cart, waggon and gears, which losses in the whole amount to £120 and upwards.

56 Abbey Green, pre-1914. The 1543 Constable Rental mentions Cole Green outside the former priory gatehouse. Mid-17th-century rentals list newly erected properties on the green, reflecting a westward expansion of the built-up area. On the left the new *Plough and Ball* is being built; to the right is the 1847 Abbey Street School and the chimney of the ribbon (later hat) factory.

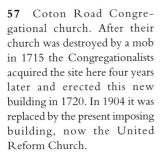

57 Coton Road Congregational church. After their church was destroyed by a mob in 1715 the Congregationalists acquired the site here four years later and erected this new building in 1720. In 1904 it was replaced by the present imposing building, now the United Reform Church.

Crime too serious for the manor court also came within the jurisdiction of Quarter Sessions. In 1663: 'John Bird of Nuneaton, John Miller of the same, butcher, John Ellis of the same, butcher, and John Webster of the same, blacksmith, indicted for a riotous assault upon one William Duffkin [Fine made by all except Bird].' John Ellis seems to have been a pugnacious character. Seven years later he made two further appearances at Warwick. First, with Daniel Whyte of Attleborough, butcher, for an assault and battery upon Humphrey Craddock, and then for assault upon Thomas Craddock. Punishment could be severe, as in a case heard in 1660: 'Anne Drakely wife of John Drakely of Attleborough indicted for stealing two pewter platters of the goods of Jarvis Buswell. Judgement: to be whipped.'

A final matter which concerned Quarter Sessions was the regulation of nonconformist churches or meeting houses. Between 1660 and 1690 official attitudes swung frequently from prohibition to toleration. During this period, three groups of dissenters have been traced in the Nuneaton area. The largest, and with the most continuous history, was the Presbyterian (later Congregational) Church. This body claimed the right to appoint its own ministers and organise its own worship. The first Presbyterian minister was Dr Robert Wild, who came to Nuneaton after ejection from Aynho, Northamptonshire, in 1662. By 1669 his congregation, which had numbered about thirty, 'had growne to 120 or more'. The meeting was not licensed in 1672 but re-appears, with John Burnham as minister, from 1693 to 1738. During his ministry the Presbyterians had a meeting house, location unknown, which was wrecked by a mob in 1715. Four years later they acquired a site near the boundary of Chilvers Coton parish in Coton Road and built a new church which was registered in 1720. Its successor, the present United Reform Church, still occupies the same site.

The General Baptists also had a small congregation in Nuneaton, first mentioned in 1669. In 1672 a mercer's warehouse belonging to William Sadler was licensed for worship. Sadler, who had previously been connected

58 Manor Court Road Baptist church. Baptists were first noted in the town in 1669 but do not seem to have flourished until after 1825. In 1840 the Baptists took over the former Samaritan Chapel in Midland Road and then in 1875 occupied a disused factory on the corner of Meadow Street. The present church dates from 1898.

with Baptists in Atherstone, had been described by William Trevis in the Grammar School tumult of 1663 'as a professed Anabaptist'. In depositions made to the Bishop's Court at Lichfield in 1675 it was alleged that William Sadler:

> Hath neither thrice, twise, nor once in eny of the years articulated ... received the holy Sacrament of Communion of the Lord's Supper aforesayd in his parish Church of Nun Eaton. But obstinately hath refused and still Doth refuse to participate in that holy Sacrament with the rest of the Congregacion to the great danger of his owne soule and the evill Example of other good Christians and noe small scandall and offence to Religion.

William's guilt or innocence has not yet come to light and the Baptists do not seem to have flourished until the early 19th century.

Despite Nuneaton's proximity to Fenny Drayton, the birthplace of George Fox, the Quakers were not well supported in the town. No Quakers appear before 1689, and no meeting house is licensed before the one in Gregory Goodall's Abbey End house in 1721 and 1726, after which nothing more is known. There is, though, a long-established Quaker meeting house in the neighbouring parish of Hartshill. Though small in numbers and uncertain in progress, nonconformity did have significance for the town. It broke the monopoly of the established church and introduced a new freedom of worship.

Seven

ENCLOSURE, INDUSTRY AND TRANSPORT IN THE 18TH CENTURY

The 17th and 18th centuries were a period of slow but highly significant economic change. In agriculture, the thousand-year-old open fields were swept away by enclosure. Industry also changed with the introduction to the area of silk ribbon weaving, while deeper coal mining encouraged the use of a more advanced technology. Allied to these changes was the development of new means of transport in the attempt to create and serve a widening market area.

The decision of the landowners to substitute compact farms with enclosed fields for the scattered holdings of open-field strips was connected to the price of corn. The two decades after 1730 produced a most unusual run of good harvests. The consequent glut of corn forced prices down, reducing returns to both landowners and tenant farmers. There was a real incentive to concentrate on non-grain products. On the heavy Midland soils, where cereal growing involved more effort and greater risk, the emphasis changed to meat and dairy products. Effective animal husbandry needed smaller enclosed fields.

The actual enclosure of Nuneaton and Attleborough open fields was scheduled to take place on 25 March 1733. But this was preceded by two years of detailed preparation. Before it could begin, a substantial majority of the freeholders of the yardlands had to be agreed on enclosure. There were some 76 yardlands involved, extending over 3,616 acres. The principal owner was Sir Thomas Aston, with 26 yardlands, followed by Lord Paget with 17 and Francis Stratford with six. Acting together, these three could easily out-vote the smaller freeholders.

Commissioners to oversee the enclosure were chosen from local Warwickshire gentry, but the vital person was the professional surveyor. This was Henry Beighton of Griff, who had to calculate the extent of the open fields furlong by furlong and to re-allocate the land in compact blocks. Beighton's plans were then approved by the Commissioners and incorporated into a private Act of Parliament which gave the freeholders legal title to their new estates.

One problem concerned tithe payable to the church on both crops and animals. Enclosure provided a good opportunity to extinguish this troublesome tax by awarding a proportion of the land to the tithe owners as a once-and-for-all payment. The right to collect tithes belonged to Sir Thomas Hoby, the lay patron of the parish, though one-third went to the vicar who also had his glebe land in the open fields. These two stood to gain greatly from enclosure. In fact, Sir Thomas was awarded 406 acres and the vicar, John Ryder, 127 acres, and they still continued to collect tithes on the remaining farmland not covered by the award. Sir Thomas Aston, Lord Paget and Francis Stratford were allocated 684, 406 and 313 acres respectively. Most of the smaller freeholders had between two and 19 acres, depending on their previous holdings.

The fate of the tenant farmers is unknown. All leases were made void by the Act so, presumably, new ones had to be negotiated with the owners. Small freeholders, whose allocations proved unviable, could lease to tenants or increase their holdings by renting extra land. Enclosure actually improved the status of the owners of certain ancient cottages, to which were attached traditional grazing rights over the open fields. Since these rights could not be exercised on the new enclosed lands, the Commissioners created the Cottagers' Piece: 113 acres of freehold grazing between Weddington Road and Higham Lane.

Nuneaton's poor were little affected by these changes since the commons to which they had access escaped enclosure in 1733. Soaring food prices in the French Wars, though, brought a fresh impetus to maximise profits. A second Enclosure Act in 1802 allowed 660 acres of common and waste to pass into private owner-ship. The only, and somewhat unwelcome, compensation for the poor was the 18 acres of common enclosed to supplement the poor rates.

If the social effects of enclosure were less than is commonly believed, the physical effect was immense. In one season the ancient prairie-type landscape of eastern Nuneaton and Attleborough completely disappeared. The same happened in Chilvers Coton in 1764. Compact, hedged and ditched fields became the norm, and new purpose-built farmhouses in the countryside replaced the ancient farms along the old streets. Our 'traditional' landscape is only some two and a half centuries old.

The landscape was also changing in the south and west of the area. With the growing demand for fuel, coal mining was experiencing a modest expansion in Coton and Stockingford. Spoil banks and abandoned shafts marked the industry's expansion across the land. Three hundred years of mining had extracted most of the coal which could be won from the out-crop. During the 17th century mining moved further into the coal field. The old bell pits were unsuitable for deeper mining and shafts had to be sunk to reach the coal seams. From Sir John Newdigate's accounts of 1603-6, it appears that a new mine shaft at Griff was some 80 feet deep. The sinkers were paid increasing amounts as the shaft passed through the Ryder and the Stone or Slate seams with a reward of 4d. for hitting the Seven Feet Coal.

Mining at these greater depths brought drainage problems. Payments were made in 1604 for: 'Making a lade hole to lade water to

59 Hinckley Road: Ensor's Farm. Enclosure of Nuneaton's open fields in 1733 not only created a new hedged landscape but also removed the ancient farmsteads from the Church Street/Bond Gate area. Farmers now had purpose-built farm-houses close to their new compact farms.

the water pit sumpe, for two laders lading water to the water pit with 1s. for candles for the laders and 1s. for 3 ould scopes to lade water with and 7s. for feing [clearing] the earth that was fallen in by reason the work was rooffed with water.' The water was brought to the surface by drains or soughs and where the land sloped, or by chains of buckets powered by horse gins. Water wheels to drive pumps were in use before 1700. These could be huge, producing considerable horsepower. At the Newdigate pits in Collycroft in 1683 there was 'a water wheel 8yds. 16ins. in diameter turned by water in a 3 in. bore pipe'. This wheel was replaced in 1701-2 by a 'great new water wheel at work'. Then the water had to be carried away from the mines. Richard Newdigate constructed a sough 453 yards long from near Griff to Heath End. Here it joined the stream running down to the brook in Wash Lane (Queen's Road) and so into the Anker by the town mill.

Technology was further advanced in 1714 when the first Newcomen atmospheric steam engine in Warwickshire was erected at Griff. Though it was crude and inefficient, consuming vast quantities of coal, the new beam engine could work continuously to pump the Griff mines dry.

Local mining, though, was not a story of continual progress. In fact, it was disjointed and littered with financial failures. Martin Bayley, who had leased mines of Sir Willoughby Aston's part of Nuneaton Common in 1692, wrote despairingly seven years later:

> I have had ... wett yeares, a thin bad Coale, powerfull and implacable enemies; Howere I have no reason to murmure when I consider my neighbours and brethren in the same trades are now lying in Goales [sic] unable to pay either Landlord or others tho' great summes are owing ...

Coal fields were closed down and re-opened throughout the period. When Sir Richard sub-let his coal lease on Lord Paget's land to James Ludford and Theodore Stratford in 1689, he

60 Griff Colliery: the atmospheric engine, 1714. Cartographer Henry Beighton made this fine drawing of the Newcomen engine erected close to his Griff home. The engine brought significant progress in drainage and enabled the sinking of deeper mines.

promised to cease mining at Griff for the ten-year duration of the lease.

Though local mining was technically advanced, failure was more common than success because too many mine owners were competing for a limited market. Poor transport was the chief problem. Coal was mainly carried by packhorse at an estimated doubling of cost every two-three miles from the pit head. The coalmasters, vainly pursuing quick profits, failed to see the need to create a wider and more stable market.

The first entrepreneur with the vision to join technology to market creation was Sir Roger Newdigate, who succeeded to Arbury in 1734. He realised the economic importance of the new (late 1750s) Bedworth-Coventry turnpike road, and backed the extension through Griff to Nuneaton. By charging tolls, turnpike trusts could provide well-made surfaced roads. A survey made in 1775 shows that Watling Street, Hinckley Road and the new Long Shoot, Lutterworth Road, the Mancetter and the

61 Coton Road tollgate cottage. After *c*.1750 all the major roads out of Nuneaton were taken over by turnpike trusts. At the entry to each section a cottage was provided for the gate-keeper who collected the tolls. This cottage on the Coton Road/Bridge Street corner was demolished in 1910.

62 Griff Hollows. The late 1750s brought the Coventry to Bedworth turnpike road which, under the influence of Sir Roger Newdigate, was extended to Nuneaton and Hinckley to widen the coal market. Here the road passes through Griff Hollows; the building on the left was originally the *Newdegate Arms* inn.

Coleshill Roads were all turnpiked. Coal could now be conveyed cheaply by wagon throughout North Warwickshire and South Leicestershire.

Sir Roger Newdigate was even quicker to see the advantages of canals for bulk transport. Within ten years of James Brindley's earliest canal—the Bridgewater of 1756—Sir Roger was cutting across the Arbury estate his own canal system, described in 1764 as 'by far the greatest length of canal belonging to an individual in the kingdom'. He was later able to connect the Arbury system to the Coventry

Canal by the Communication Canal in 1773. By 1778 the seams near Collycroft were exhausted and the colliery had to be resited to the north near the later Bermuda village. This necessitated a new canal link, the Griff Hollows Canal of the early 1790s.

Sir Roger, with fellow coalmaster Richard Parrot of Hawkesbury, was an active promoter of the Coventry Canal Bill. On 10 August 1769 the first section of the new navigation—from Bedworth to the city—was opened with typical celebrations by the inhabitants. According to

63 Chilvers Coton: the *Boot Inn*, *c.*1928. Wherever boats stopped at wharves canal-side public houses soon appeared. Coton had two in close proximity: the *Wharf* and *Boot* inns. Across the road from the *Boot* were stables and warehousing. The old inn was replaced by the present building around 1937.

64 Chilvers Coton: the old Cat Gallows Bridge, pre-1914. Where the canal crossed the existing footpath from Heath End towards the town, the company had to maintain the way. This footbridge was replaced in 1914 with one offering easier access. The origin of the name remains conjectural.

the *Coventry Mercury*: 'Two boats, with Coals, were brought up to this City, from the side of Bedworth. As these were the first that ever made the passage, they were received with loud Huzzas by the people assembled to see them.' Their enthusiasm, however, was to prove somewhat premature. The canal had only reached Atherstone by 1771, when the company exhausted its capital. After lengthy legal battles, the section from Fazeley to Fradley Junction was constructed by the Birmingham & Fazeley and the Trent & Mersey Companies. The

Coventry Company then raised a mortgage to link Atherstone to Fazeley and the project was finally completed in July 1790.

But the Coventry Canal, like the turnpike roads, only served the local area. Sir Roger had a greater vision: a waterway to London. He was an active promoter of the 1769 Oxford Canal Act, investing over £3,000 in the company. The canal was to run from Longford, north of Coventry, to Oxford where it would link with the Thames and so with the Capital. The vision failed to become reality. The Newcastle ship

65 *Above left*, the Griff Hollows Canal, 1930s. Part of the network of private canals planned by Sir Roger Newdigate, the Griff Hollows Canal linked the early Griff collieries with the Coventry Canal. The young Mary Ann Evans played here with her brother Isaac, and in her novels re-named it 'Red Deeps'.

66 *Above right*, Coton Road Weir, pre-1896.

owners, who feared the loss of their coal monopoly, inserted a clause into the Oxford Bill which forbade carrying coal by water beyond Oxford. The venture did prove a partial success. The canal reached Banbury by 1778 and Oxford in 1790, widening the coal market to the South Midlands. Before the end of the century the Griff mines were adding up to £4,000 yearly to Arbury's income. Paradoxically, though, the new canals led to a decline in Warwickshire coal after 1800. Staffordshire coalmasters used the canal system to capture first the Coventry and then the Oxford markets. The Warwickshire coalfield had to await the development of a railway system before its resources could be fully exploited.

The Arbury Connection

No account of the Nuneaton area would be complete without reference to its finest architectural jewel, Arbury Hall. But Arbury has other significant associations through its connection to three of the most famous people born in the area: Henry Beighton, Sir Roger Newdigate and Mary Ann Evans. Two of them, Beighton and Newdigate, spent most of their lives at or close to Arbury; Mary Ann Evans only found fame after she had left the area.

Some thirty years after the former Arbury Priory had passed to the Duke of Suffolk, it was bought by a rising London lawyer, Edmund Anderson, who 'totally demolished the old fabrick of the House and Church and built out of their ruins a very fair structure in quadrangular form'. When Anderson became Chief Justice of the Court of Common Pleas, in 1582, he sought a residence nearer to London and exchanged Arbury in 1586 for Harefield Place, Middlesex, the seat of John Newdegate whose family had its origins in the village of Newdigate in Surrey. By the 17th century the family spelt their name as Newdigate, too, but Frances Parker reverted to Newdegate in 1806.

In 1642 the owner of Arbury was Richard Newdigate, grandson of John, who was made a judge in 1655 and, briefly, Chief Justice after Cromwell's death in 1658. Returning to his law practice he became sufficiently wealthy to buy back Harefield and also purchase the castle and manor of Astley adjoining Arbury. Created baronet in 1677, Sir Richard died the following year, and was succeeded by his eldest son, Sir Richard II, to whom Arbury had passed a few years earlier. Richard built the splendid stable block at Arbury around 1674, with its porch designed by Sir Christopher Wren, and the sumptuously carved chapel in the house in 1678.

During Sir Richard's time, Henry Beighton was born at Chilvers Coton on 20 August 1687. As son of a farming family, Henry grew up with a keen appreciation of the local landscape and was well aware of the changes as Sir Richard developed mining techniques on his estate. To become a surveyor was the obvious choice and he gained early practice working for Sir Richard in both Bedworth and Nuneaton. One of his early interests was the weather and the accurate records he kept were sent to the Royal Society, to which he was elected member, in London. Among his records was

An Account of a Most Terrible Hurricane at Nun-Eaton in Warwickshire The 29th August and Next Morning … Before its reaching Nun-Eaton It came over part of the Parish of Chilvers Coton (where I live) and in its way at the breadth of about 40 or 50 yards Took down all the branches of the Trees before it,

and where there was much Timber It cut a Perfect Avenue of that Breadth …

Merrys house Three bays of Timber building was all crushed inward into the Body of the Building and a Tyled house or Barn Stripped …

Then it Entered in to the Market Square where stood a Cage or Wood prison 7 feet Square and 7 foot to the Wall plate Was Blown up and carryed some yards towards the wind with the Stocks Wiping Post and Pillory …

Thomas Smiths House all stripped and most part unroofed it fell on the people in Bed in a Parlour, who were Saved by the Bed posts being very strong, from Whence they crept through a hole and got out …

And here the Hurricane Left the Town and entred the open Field, many pieces of Glass windows were found at half a mile distance.

In 1714 Henry Beighton became editor of the *Ladies' Diary, or The Women's Almanac,* designed to interest women in scientific and literary matters, a post he held for the remainder of his life. He also showed skills in the new technology, designing a new improved valve for the Newcomen Engine at Washington Colliery near Newcastle. In about 1720 he announced his greatest project, a new and accurately surveyed map of Warwickshire. The survey was completed by late 1725 and the map engraved and delivered to subscribers in 1728. Beighton was in demand as an enclosure surveyor, made maps and drawings for the 1730 edition of *Dugdale's Antiquities,* and even found time to letter the fine charity boards in Coton church before his death in 1743.

Richard died in 1710 and was succeeded by two sons who both left no issue before his youngest son Roger became the owner of Arbury at the age of 14 in 1734. Roger was educated at Oxford which he followed with a Grand Tour of Europe, returning with an informed cultural education which led to the transformation of Arbury.

For the next ten years Sir Christopher [Roger] was occupied with the architectural metamorphosis of his old family mansion, thus antici-

67 Arbury Hall. Originally a Tudor brick mansion, Arbury was gothicised by Sir Roger Newdigate after 1750. With its stone skin, traceried windows, crenellated battlements and elaborate plasterwork interior, it has survived unchanged as the best example of an early Gothic Revival mansion.

pating, through the prompting of his individual taste, that general reaction from the insipid imitation of the Palladian style towards a restoration of the Gothic.

[George Eliot, *Mr. Gilfil's Love Story*]

The transformation of the interior, room by room, started in 1750 and continued under three successive architects during the next half century, creating a fantasy of Gothic vaulting and tracery in plaster. The exterior, too, was given a skin of stone, crenellated battlements and cloisters around the yard, while the formal gardens were replaced by an informally wild landscape. Sir Roger's legacy was the best example of a Gothic Revival house to remain intact and unchanged up to the present day.

Builder, entrepreneur and Member of Parliament for 35 years (first for Middlesex and then Oxford), Sir Roger still found time for involvement in local affairs. As principal landowner he was obviously concerned in the enclosure of Chilvers Coton in 1764 and, again, in 1770 in Bedworth, where he had two yardlands and was also a governor of the Nicholas Chamberlaine Charity, which owned half the open fields.

On Friday 20 September 1766 some two hundred Bedworth miners had marched on Coventry where they suspected the cheese factors had created a shortage to raise prices. They had forcibly taken loads of cheese, which they sold in open market at the old price, returning the money to the owners. The following day the miners marched on Nuneaton market and riot was only avoided by the prompt intervention of Sir Roger. Jopson's *Coventry Mercury* reported:

The Inhabitants of Nuneaton think it their Indispensible Duty to return (In this Public Manner) their sincere thanks to Sir Roger Newdigate Bart. ... and the rest of the Gentlemen for their kind and friendly Interposition on Saturday last. Sir Roger Newdigate Bart. Ordered some hundred weight of his own Cheese to be sold at the Market there at 2½d per pound; and several Farmers brought Bags of Wheat (a Thing not seen there for several Years past).

Perhaps Sir Roger's most enduring monument in the village was the erection in 1800 of a new workhouse, grandly named the Chilvers Coton College for the Poor. This grimly huge stone block dominated the village. It is possible that Sir Roger's intentions were benevolent—

George Eliot in *Amos Barton* saw it as a refuge—but, after it became the Union Workhouse for the whole Nuneaton District following the 1834 Poor Law Act, it was regarded as a place of harsh servitude.

Sir Roger died in 1806 without issue, thus ending the baronetcy, and Arbury passed to a distant cousin, Francis Parker, who adopted the Newdegate surname. The *Nuneaton Diary* writer, who was patently biased against the Tories, wrote a bitter obituary when Francis Parker Newdegate died in 1835:

> Death of F. Newdegate Esq. Of Arbury Hall at Leamington in his 85th year after having possessed the Arbury Estate for 29 years. Said to have died worth half a million of Money. He was a dispisable character—a bad unfeeling Landlord—a notorious violator of his words and promises, particularly with his Tenantry who he ejected from his farms without Mercy. Universally hated as a tyrant ought to be and detested by the honest who knew him of all parties.

When Francis Parker first came to Arbury he brought his young land agent from Kirk Hallam, Derbyshire to manage the estate. Thus came Robert Evans to South Farm, Arbury, where his fifth surviving child, Mary Ann, was born 13 years later on 22 November 1819. Mary Ann, whose mother was Robert's second wife, Christiana Pearson of Astley, was to become George Eliot, the one undoubted genius born in the Nuneaton area.

Mary Ann Evans was given the education befitting the daughter of a professional family. Three years old, she went with her brother Isaac to a dame school near Griff House (to which the family had moved in 1820) and became a boarder at Miss Latham's school in Attleborough two years later. In 1828 she moved to the superior school run by Mrs Wallington at The Elms, Vicarage Street, Nuneaton. After three years she went to the school in Coventry run by the Misses Franklin, where she stayed until her mother died in 1836 and she became housekeeper to her father.

In 1841 Robert Evans retired to Foleshill. During this period Mary Ann abandoned her fervently evangelical religious beliefs, causing a family split. Reconciled to her father, Mary Ann remained with him until his death in 1849. The misery of this decade was only made bearable by the friendship of Charles Bray and his family, which opened up new intellectual horizons to this impressionable young woman.

68 South Farm, Arbury. This was Robert Evans' first home when he came to Nuneaton to manage the Arbury estate for Francis Parker Newdegate. Here was born his daughter Mary Ann, who was to achieve fame as George Eliot.

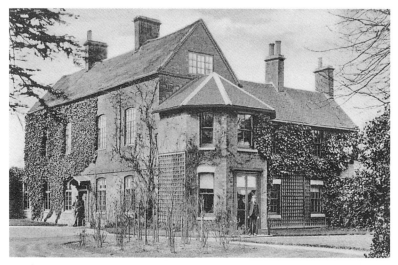

69 Griff House. When Mary Ann was eight months old, the Evans family moved to Griff House, which remained her home for the next 22 years. A much more imposing residence than South Farm, it reflected Robert Evans' growing status. The house is now part of a hotel with extensive modern additions.

70 The Elms, Vicarage Street. Nine-year-old Mary Ann Evans went to board for three years at Mrs Wallington's school, The Elms, where she received an excellent grounding in education. The house was badly damaged in the 1941 air raid and later demolished for the new Magistrates' Court.

Released from her Warwickshire ties, Mary Ann finally settled in London, where her long association with George Lewes began. In 1856 *Scenes of Clerical Life* was published and Mary Ann Evans became George Eliot. The setting of the three *Scenes* was her part of Warwickshire, where Chilvers Coton became Shepperton and Nuneaton Milby: 'It was a dingy-looking town with a strong smell of tanning up one street and a great shaking of hand-looms up another.' (*Janet's Repentance*)

This was not the Nuneaton of 1856. *Amos Barton* and *Janet's Repentance* are both set some thirty years earlier, while *Mr. Gilfil* looks back to the time of Sir Roger Newdigate. In all three *Scenes* the events are real and the characters closely drawn from prominent local people and her own relatives. Behind the fiction lies a remarkable feat of memory backed by pains-taking research. Most of her novels share the same characteristics. The recurring themes are of conflicting family relationships and crises of conscience, and a firm sense of place, which mirrors the author's early life. George Eliot may have exchanged her Nuneaton past for literary London life, but it was her experiences in Warwickshire which remained her constant inspiration.

Eight

THE RISE AND DECLINE
OF THE SILK RIBBON TRADE

Coventry's great woollen cloth industry began to decline in the 16th century, with a corresponding effect on the neighbouring area. Coventry merchants sought a replacement textile product and found silk. Presumably the availability of weaving skills made it worth importing raw silk from southern Europe via London to the English Midlands. A Silk Weavers Company was established in Coventry by 1627. The usual pattern occurred with the trade spreading to Bedworth, Nuneaton and the local villages.

The earliest recorded silk weaver in Nuneaton is William Oswin, who died in 1659. His probate inventory lists 'all the implements in the Shop belonging to his trade and worke made and silke Redy to worke up in the house: £37'. The first inventory specifically mentioning silk ribbon weaving is that of Andrew Randall who died on Christmas Day 1662. He was working on a large scale with looms, a warp mill and silk valued at £180. His widow Grace continued the business for a further twenty years. Her inventory (1682) is significant for two reasons. In the first place it refers to 'silk in the workmens hands', which is possible evidence for the putting out system. Secondly, the business may have been failing with Letters of Administration granted to her principal creditors, both London merchants. The London connection, a significant feature of the ribbon trade, was already in existence.

Much has been made of the influence of French protestant refugees—the Huguenots—who fled to England following the revocation of the Edict of Nantes in 1685. Being weavers, they settled in textile areas, including Coventry. They have been credited with the introduction of ribbon weaving, though it patently pre-dates

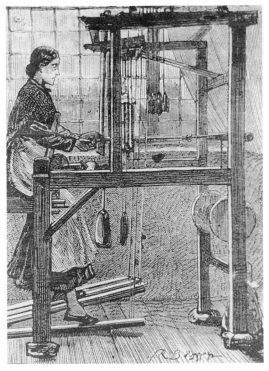

71 A handloom weaver. This sketch shows handloom weaving in the era of the domestic system. Prominent is the typically large window which enabled the weaver to maximise daylight working.

their arrival. Evidence is often cited for names of French origin in this area but, again, names like Jacques and Mallabone appear a century or more earlier. Neither is there a sudden increase of new French names post-1685 in Nuneaton and Bedworth parish registers. Huguenots did set up weaving sheds in Kenilworth Castle ruins and they may have introduced new techniques, but silk ribbon weaving was firmly rooted in the locality for half a century before 1685.

The ribbon trade had a three-tier structure. Dominating the industry was a small group of master merchants. By 1800 there were probably twelve or so in Coventry, four in Nuneaton and one in Bedworth. The merchants had to be men of substance. They had warehouses locally and in London, imported the raw silk, and had it thrown (spun) and dyed. The silk was then passed on to the middle-men or undertakers. These distributed the silk to groups of weavers who wove the ribbon and were paid two-thirds of the finished price. The merchants then sent the ribbon to London by packhorse or, later, by canal for the retail trade. The handloom weavers formed the base. Theirs was a domestic industry. Weavers' cottages had extra large windows to enable as much work as possible to be done by daylight. The whole family had jobs. Adults did the weaving, while children had such tasks as silk winding, preparing the warp, shuttle-filling and picking-up. Census returns show that elderly people reverted to these childhood tasks when they could no longer weave.

Most weavers used the single handloom. This could only weave single ribbons but a skilled weaver could produce the most intricate work. From around 1770 the Dutch Engine Loom was introduced. Despite its name it was still a handloom, but it could produce several plain ribbons at a time. The Jacquard Loom was introduced into Coventry by the 1820s. This

72 College Street: handloom weavers' houses, 1970. The dwellings of domestic industry workers could be identified by their unusually large windows. This block was demolished when the Bedworth by-pass was extended to Nuneaton.

73 Regent Street: ribbon weavers' tenement block. One development of domestic industry was the topshop, where the work space was above the house. This purpose-built block must be pre-1850 since factory weaving became dominant after that time.

used needles operated by punched cards, allowing one operator to produce several patterned ribbons. The outlying districts were too poor to install Jacquard Looms, and the best work could still only be done on handlooms.

Entry to the trade was by serving a seven-year apprenticeship. This was followed by a period as a journey-man (day-paid) weaver. During this time, the journey-man would hope to save sufficient money to buy a loom and set up as a master weaver. The best a weaver could achieve was to become an undertaker employing his own group of weaving families. The gulf between undertaker and capitalist master merchant was impossibly great.

The stable pattern of the ribbon trade was disrupted by the French Wars of 1793-1815. Many weavers enlisted and the shortfall was made up by 'half-pay' apprentices, children who were put to weaving on low pay. London silk houses were eager to bypass the master merchants by directly financing undertakers to set up workshops. Wartime prosperity brought a boom to the trade, especially 1813-15, the 'Big Purl Time'. The boom proved to be short-lived. Post-war depression led to over-production and reduced prices. The *Nuneaton Diary*—a record of local events probably written by John Astley—noted the changing situation: 'August 1815. This month and the former the ribbon trade rather flat, the warehouses being stocked with goods, the trade reduced the price for making those goods which they had latterly given such unprecedented high prices for.' In March 1817, at the depth of the depression: 'The Society in London for the Relief of the Suffering Poor gave £200 and 100 blankets to the Committee here for their distribution.'

The trade reacted to the worsening situation with an agreed list of prices for weaving but the small masters with tight margins were ready to undercut them. Nuneaton weavers, though, had their own methods of enforcing the agreement: '18th August 1819. A donkey with a man upon his back, face towards the tail, was conducted through the streets by a group of men and boys of the lowest class. The man [Flyde] mounted being charged with working at a depressed price. Two others, Ellis and Kent, were conducted in like manner.' That day and the next the town was in a state of agitated confusion and near drama, as the diarist recorded:

> The Cryer in his official capacity requested a Meeting of the undertakers and journeymen weavers at the top of Abby Street at 9 o'clock in the morning to consider on the best manner for adjusting the prices ... Shortly afterwards the Cryer ordered by the Constable to request the inhabitants not to attend until the Coventry prices had been adjusted.

> 19th August 1819. No meeting of any consequence took place at the top of Abby Street as requested the previous evening but large assemblies of weavers were standing about, having struck for a regulation price according to list made in 1816. Some of the lowest class proceeded through the streets insisting upon people whom they found at work to leave off till their demands were granted which was generally complied with.

> Mr. Craddock thought it necessary to send to Capt. Ludford, Ansley, for the Yeomanry Cavalry, part of whom equipped themselves and was proceeding towards the town until met by a messenger stating their services were not required.

From 1824 onwards the silk trade faced a new threat. Imports of foreign ribbons had been banned from Britain by Acts of 1761 and 1771. But government policy now favoured free trade. In February 1824 the Chancellor proposed to allow silk ribbon imports, a move which the local trade feared would be disastrous. The weavers reacted by sending several petitions to

the House of Commons. The proposal was delayed and modified. From 1826 imports were allowed, but with a duty of 25-40 per cent. The initial effect was slight—plentiful work at lower prices—but from October 1828 the situation deteriorated:

> *February 1829*. Ribbon Trade continues bad. The looms not more than half employed since about October last. Prices greatly reduced.

> *March 1829*. The Ribbon Trade continues wretchedly bad. The year's Poor Rates amounted to 5s.6d. in pound.

The slump continued into the winter of 1830, when volunteers opened a charitable soup kitchen dispensing 140 gallons a day to the poor. 1831 was even worse. According to an official report, Nuneaton had 2,072 looms, with 4,087 workers available, of whom 2,496 (61 per cent) were unemployed. The soup kitchen re-opened, now dispensing 700 gallons weekly, and 2,700 persons were on parish poor relief. Distressed weavers expressed their resentment by breaking 200 windows in silk warehouses, factories and dwellings. Violence was only halted by the prompt swearing-in of 250 special constables.

The Coventry area, already under threat from imported ribbon, faced the further problem of technical backwardness. Silk towns in north-west England were already using steam power: Congleton, Leek and Derby together had 586 power looms; Coventry a mere 53. Complacency was a major factor in this retardation, but social considerations were also important. The self-employed handloom weavers valued their independence and authority. They had always kept irregular hours, never working on 'Saint Monday' (and even 'Saint Tuesday'!) then toiling throughout the nights to complete the weekly quota. Steam power meant factory work, with the loss of status and the replacement of traditional skills by machines. When Josiah Beck opened the first steam mill in Coventry in 1831 rioting weavers destroyed the machinery and burned down the building.

74 Abbey Street: ribbon factory, 1967. The *Nuneaton Diary* has several references to building a ribbon factory above an existing house. This allowed small entrepreneurs to employ several handloom workers, a stage in the move from domestic to powered factory employment.

75 Abbey Street: Ebery's ribbon factory, 1968. Here the ribbon factory has been erected at the rear of an existing cottage. This small workshop could accommodate some six hand-looms. The building ended its days as a taxi business.

The introduction of factory weaving to Nuneaton was less dramatic but hardly more effective. In 1830 the *Diary* records a steam mill in Attleborough, possibly Jacombs' mill, selling off 17 Jacquard Looms in 1833 and going bankrupt in 1834. A year later the parish decided to set up its own mill in Wheat Street to provide the unemployed with work. This also failed, according to a government report of 1840, and was 'an injudicious tampering with trade and industry by the parish authorities'. In January 1836 Barnwell's steam factory opened, also at the top of Wheat Street. Whether this was the failed parish project under new ownership or a new mill is not clear. It was followed in 1844 by Messrs Greatrex & Taverner's mill in Oddaways or Horeston Lane (now Oaston Road). This was enlarged a year later to house 96 looms. Other known silk factories were on the sites later occupied by the Hall & Phillips and Abbey Green hat factories. John Earp also had a silk factory at the Hermitage in Galley Common.

Opposition to factory work was still strong, however, and an attempt was made in 1858 to

76   The Albion Buildings, Attleborough Road. After *c.*1850 the handloom trade was facing opposition from factory weaving, which was opposed by the handloom weavers who prized their independence. The 1858 Albion Buildings marked an ingenious solution: traditional weavers' houses and topshops, but powered by steam. In 1860 the top storey was taken over by Thomas Townsend's for cotton spinning.

combine domestic and factory industry: the Albion Buildings in Attleborough Road was a three-storied building with weaving topshops above the workers' dwellings. The significant difference from the usual weavers' tenements was the steam engine house at the end of the row which turned a power shaft running the length of the top storey. The weavers paid steam rent and could retain their traditional independence while enjoying the new advantages of steam production.

This ingenious experiment, unfortunately, had only a brief existence. The year 1860 brought the completion of free trade. Foreign silk ribbon could now enter the country duty-free. The Coventry weavers made one last stand with a 12-week strike to maintain prices. When they were forced back to work, they were met by empty order books and a trade set for permanent decline. For Nuneaton, too, over two centuries of silk weaving was coming to a sad but inevitable end.

Nine

POPULATION, PROBLEMS AND PROGRESS IN THE MID-19TH CENTURY

The first national population census was taken in 1801. Successive censuses became more refined, adding more information including birth places for the first time in 1851. The information was compiled by census enumerators who each visited some 200 households. Their returns became public a hundred years later and demographic historians were quick to exploit this new source from the 1950s onwards. Locally, research has concentrated on Nuneaton town, still covering substantially the same area it did in the Tudor period. The returns yield a total population of 5,135 inhabitants living in 1,221 households—an average of 4.2 persons per household. Household sizes ranged from one to 17 with the vast majority (969 or 79.4 per cent) between two and six persons, nearly double today's but not really large.

One major difference from today is the age structure. This was predominantly a young population with 34.2 per cent under 15 years and 94.1 per cent under 65 years of age. The reasons for this youth bias must be related to the terrible sanitary conditions and the generally low standard of living. Only 146 men and 151 women had survived to the modern pensionable age. Having survived more than six decades, this remaining 5 per cent had proved remarkably resistant to their environment.

When the inhabitants are divided into industrial and social groups, another important contrast appears. Nuneaton in 1851 had a much greater working population. Just over 60 per cent were in full or part-time work. When wives and children under 15 at work are deducted from their industrial groups, the proportion drops to just over 40 per cent, much closer to the modern level. Nearly half of the working population (46 per cent) was engaged in the silk ribbon trade. Other major groups were skilled crafts (14.7 per cent), traders (9.6 per cent), agriculture (5.7 per cent), service trades and labourers (7.5 per cent). Domestic service, almost non-existent today, accounted for another 9.2 per cent. One group which is surprisingly low is coal mining and quarrying. Only 25 miners lived in the town itself and even in Stockingford, on the coal seams, there were just 36 miners recorded. Even though Nuneaton was just entering the railway age, mining was still small-scale.

Birthplace information—the new feature of the 1851 census—showed that one-third (1,707 people) were not born within the town area, though 276 of them were born elsewhere within the modern borough boundaries. As might be expected, the great majority of those born elsewhere came from Warwickshire, Leicestershire and Staffordshire, and migration was largely from within a 20-mile radius of the town. Domestic servants were usually recruited from the surrounding farming villages because:

There is the greatest difficulty in prevailing upon parents to let their children come to service. The young women look down with scorn upon it. As housewives there are none worse. They can neither make nor mend their own clothes; they cannot sew; they know nothing of domestic management; they cannot make a house comfortable and the men, not expecting it, seek the beer shops.

[*Handloom Weavers Report* 1840]

Even so, birthplaces are found among most English counties, Scotland, Wales, Ireland and abroad. The curate of St Nicolas Church had children born in Smyrna (Izmir, Turkey) and one inhabitant was born on a ship rounding the Cape of Good Hope!

The low expectation of life suggested by the census is borne out by the Health Report of 1848. The Public Health Act of that year allowed local areas to form a Board of Health where the death rate exceeded 27 per thousand or where 10 per cent of the ratepayers

77 An Abbey Street Court. The growth of the ribbon trade brought the first large population increase. This was met by building courtyards of houses down the long medieval burgage plots. Small, overcrowded, lacking light, piped water and sewage disposal, the courts produced the appalling conditions described in the 1848 Health Report.

petitioned for a board. Nuneaton qualified on both counts. In December 1848 the Central Board sent an inspector, George Clark, to Nuneaton to survey the town. In his report Mr Clark set down the root cause of the town's sanitary problems: the lack of any efficient local authority. The manor court had fallen into disuse and the parish vestry of annually changing churchwardens and overseers could not cope with the growing town.

In nearly two hundred years since the Hearth Tax the population had more than trebled. This increase was not reflected in a larger built-up area. Instead, landlords had built courtyards of small houses on the long plots behind the town streets.

> In these places the greater part of the population are lodged in courts communicating with the street by a narrow covered entry and open to the fields behind. They consist of from 5 to 15 houses each, with one or two privies in common, a large open tank or cesspool; a pump is generally very near the cesspool, often a pigstye…
>
> The cesspool is the greatest evil and the most constantly present. It is often 10 to 20 feet square and very deep. Into it are discharged the contents of the privy, and all the rubbish and filth of every kind from the houses. It is emptied only once or twice annually, and is in consequence often heaped up far above the top of its side walls, so as to expose a greatly increased offensive service.

The only drinking water supply, heavily polluted by its adjacent cesspool, was pumped from the well in each court. For washing:

> the rain water is collected in tanks … or by the poorest in pans set under the spouts and eaves of the roof. As the condition of these roof surfaces is for the most part foul, the water is of a dirty quality, as well as deficient in quantity; in which case the poor either remain unwashed or use hard water at a considerable expense in soda and soap.

George Clark remorselessly catalogued all the deficiencies of the town. The house slops were emptied into the yard or into the street;

78 St Paul's Church, Stockingford, 1904. As the silk trade and extractive industries expanded, so Stockingford became a populous village. Because of the distance from Nuneaton parish church, it became necessary to build a chapel of ease, St Paul's, in 1826.

the new gasworks was unprosperous and the streets unlit; the only burial ground was St Nicolas churchyard, recently extended but still overfull with bodies interred at ground level in brick vaults. The inspector summed up in one devastating paragraph:

> The present state of the town I found to be the subject of universal complaint. The darkness adds materially to the labours of the police, and promotes various gross immoralities. These, the darkness itself and the dirty condition of the public ways combine to render Nuneaton a place through which a respectable female could not safely walk after nightfall.

The report's recommendations were modest. The problem of the courts seemed intractable. Clark advocated the construction of sewers to take effluent into the Anker downstream of the town and suggested that Ceeswood Pool could provide a piped water supply. It would take a half century of gradual change before conditions improved materially.

According to the 1840 *Handloom Weavers Report*, the moral and spiritual condition of the inhabitants was almost as debased as the physical. The blame was laid on the often non-resident Anglican vicars: 'officiating only by curates, frequently removing, who cannot have that permanent acquaintance with, or exercise that

permanent influence upon, the mass of the population.' Even the higher clergy neglected their duties as the Nuneaton diarist recorded in July 1816:

> The new Burying ground consecrated by Dr. Cornwallis, the Bishop of Litchfield and Coventry who afterwards performed the rite of Confirmation to 1022 females and 505 males which had not been done in Nuneaton for more than 60 years. Many people attended and many went away (who purposely came for it) unconfirmed, they expecting that a second party would be confirmed after the Church was cleared of the first, which was not the case.

But change, however slowly, was under way. Both Stockingford and Attleborough had rapidly increasing populations and additional churches became a matter of urgency. New districts were carved out of the old St Nicolas parish for St Paul's Stockingford in 1826 and for Holy Trinity Attleborough in 1842.

The old dissenting churches fared little better. The Baptists remained small in number but the Congregationalists were sufficiently strong to rebuild their Coton Road church in 1793. In 1816, though, they suffered a split when the minister and part of the congregation left to form the new Zion Chapel in Bond Gate.

79 Holy Trinity Church, Attleborough. Though Attleborough village was within walking distance of St Nicolas, the size of the village brought the need for a separate church, which was met in 1842 by the erection of Holy Trinity, brick-built in the Early English style.

80 The Manse, Bond Gate. When the Coton Road Congregational church split in 1816, the secessionists built Zion Chapel to the rear of the Bond Gate properties. This elegant house was the minister's manse. It was demolished in favour of an undistinguished office block.

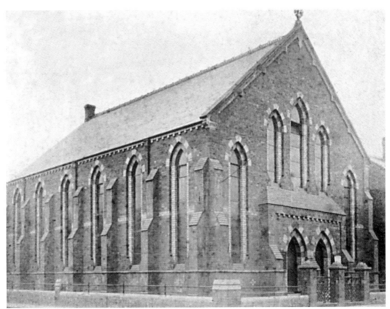

81 Abbey Street/Stratford Street Methodist church. When the first Abbey Street Methodist church became too small, it was replaced by this Early English-style chapel in 1873. Poorly designed and constructed, it had to be rebuilt in 1881 through the generosity of Reginald Stanley.

New dissent was represented by Methodism. John Wesley is reported as preaching from a window of the old *Newdegate Arms*, and the earliest chapel was built at Coton. A second church was formed in Nuneaton in 1820 and a few years later two Abbey Street cottages on the later St John's Church site were converted into a chapel. The Primitive Methodists broke away in 1851 and built their own chapel in Stratford Street. It took twenty years for Wesleyan numbers to recover and, aided by wealthy incomers including grocer J. Roberts and industrialist Reginald Stanley, they were able to build a new church on the Stratford Street/Abbey Street corner in 1873. Badly designed and constructed, it had to be rebuilt in 1881 before serving for the next eighty years.

After centuries of suppression, Roman Catholics came back to the town in 1837 when the foundation stone of their new church was laid on the Coton Road site.

The story of education mirrored that of religion, to which it was so closely allied. Until the early 18th century King Edward's remained the only public day school. Its scope was very limited, with only a dozen or so boys in the

upper school and perhaps three times as many in the lower, numbers which remained static for the next 150 years.

Public education for the working classes came about mainly through charities. In 1712 Richard Smith of Westminster left property in Nuneaton 'for and toward the clothing and educating of such poor children as should then live in the parish of Nuneaton in such manner as his then trustees should think fit'. In 1716 Smith's Charity School was built on land between the Market Place and Mill Walk. A second charity, Coton Free School, was founded in 1745 by Elizabeth, Lady Newdigate and still survives as the Coton Centre. By 1840 the Roman Catholics had started a day school in Coton Road next to their new church.

These schools could only educate small numbers of the children: Smith's 120, Coton 150, the Catholics 50 children. For the rest the only provision was private schools. The 1840 Handloom Weavers Report lists some 31 such schools, though it omitted the most expensive which did not cater for weavers' children. The quality of schooling varied enormously. At one end of the scale, the Misses Wallingford's school was sufficiently good to educate the young

82   Coton Free School, Avenue Road. Founded in 1745 for the children of All Saints Church, the original stone building was extended as a National School and remained in use until after the Second World War. After a period as the Parks Department depot it faced demolition, but was saved by local people and survives as the Coton Heritage Centre.

83   Stockingford Church School, 1960. The Rev. Robert Savage was energetic in building church schools—four in three years—in his parish. This school in Church Road, built in 1846, was demolished in the 1960s though the head teacher's house survives.

84 The National School, Attleborough Road, *c.*1902. Another of Robert Savage's schools, this one dates from 1848. Partly destroyed by war damage, the surviving buildings had a new life as the Trinity Centre before becoming commercial premises.

85 Vicarage Street School. The remaining two Savage schools were Abbey Street (1847) and this one in Vicarage Street (1848).

86   The College for the Poor, College Street, 1968. This forbidding stone block was provided in 1800 by Sir Roger Newdigate as the parish workhouse. After 1834 it became the Union Workhouse for Nuneaton and Chilvers Coton, a role it fulfilled until 1948. As the George Eliot Hospital expanded, the old workhouse, apart from the infirmary, was demolished in 1971.

George Eliot. At the other came the dame schools, little more than child minders, typified by Mrs White of Coton who told the commissioner: 'I has the Bible and Prayer-Book, and reads myself, and tells them tales like; they are so young. No books.' Last came the Sunday Schools. As well as religion, they did offer the chance for those children who worked all week to learn reading and possibly writing. For example, Coton Wesleyan Sunday School had 'Bibles, Testaments, Reading made easy and spelling books'.

It is difficult to gauge the quantity, even less the quality, but from the 1840 report it can be estimated that 1,763 out of a probable 3,500 children in the district attended some kind of school at some time. The report suggests that many children went to school when trade was slow and worked when trade was brisk. The 1840s brought substantial change. The Rev. Robert Savage, vicar of Nuneaton from 1845, totally changed educational provision in the town. In three years, funded by the Anglican National Society, he built four church schools: Stockingford in 1846, Abbey Green in 1847, and Vicarage Street and Attleborough in 1848. Though low fees still excluded the poorest, elementary education became available for the majority. Given the static population totals between 1850 and 1890, the problem was largely solved for the next forty years.

Ten

RAILWAYS AND ECONOMIC CHANGE 1840-1914

Following the success of the 1829 Liverpool-Manchester Railway the country was hit by railway mania, from which the Nuneaton area was not exempt. The author of the *Nuneaton Diary* recorded plans in 1836 for three local railway projects: a Rugby-Stafford line, Birmingham to Derby and the Grand Junction Railway. But before any of these ventures got beyond the planning stage, the national economy fell into depression and all these projects came to an abrupt halt. As the economic situation revived post-1842, so did the railway projects. In September 1844 surveys began for the proposed Trent Valley line from Rugby to Stafford via Nuneaton. Linking with this was a second project, the Coventry, Bedworth and Nuneaton Railway, which aimed to raise £90,000 by £25 shares. The Trent Valley Company, whose Act was passed in July 1845, had to raise £1,250,000.

The *Nuneaton Diary* records how the work progressed:

August 1845. Mr. Alexander, Civil Engineer, is staking out the Line by here for the Trent Valley Railway.

September 1845. On the Trent Valley line the centre of the line is marked by cutting a continuous line in the turf.

October 1845. [The contractors] have made a start by erecting works here for making Waggons etc.

November 1845. It is said that the Trent Valley Railway have agreed with Mr. Robinson for

the purchase of his land in the Bond End for £500 an acre. The Contractors have also agreed for Swinerton Timber Yard for two years and bought of him perhaps a couple of thousand pounds worth of Timber. The yard is now litterally [*sic*] speaking covered over with Workmen, Workshops and Sawpits making Waggons, Barrows etc.

The cutting of the first Sod on the Trent Valley Railway was done by Sir Robert Peel, Bart. M.P. on the 13th inst.

The Trent Valley Railway, 49 miles long, was completed in a mere 22 months. The company announced that on and after 15 September 1847 two trains would run in each direction. It was now possible to breakfast in Nuneaton and lunch in London—or take early tea in Liverpool or Manchester. For local people, the world had suddenly and dramatically become smaller.

Construction of the Nuneaton-Coventry Railway started in July 1847 and the line opened on 12 September 1850, by which date both companies had merged with the much larger London & North Western Railway. The new railway routes, though, only had a marginal effect on the local economy. In the early years, locomotive power was so limited that bulk transport was relatively expensive. The local extractive industries continued to use the canals, which cut tolls to retain trade.

The Birmingham-Leicester route was to prove much more significant. Although two projects for this route were recorded in the *Nuneaton Diary* by 1845, the line to Hinckley

87 Trent Valley railway station, 1847. The company which built the Rugby-Nuneaton-Stafford line designed many of its buildings to resemble familiar buildings, perhaps to reassure anxious passengers. Nuneaton's earliest station had, from the forecourt, the air of a country manor house. It was replaced by a more imposing building in 1876.

88 Chilvers Coton railway station. The Nuneaton-Coventry line opened in 1850 with this station as the first stop. During the war years and after the station was very busy morning and evening with workers in the Coventry factories. The slack daytime service gave the staff ample time to garden. Here they are receiving the award for the best-kept station in the region.

did not open till 1862 and to Leicester till 1864. In the latter year the Midland Railway, which had running rights over the Leicester line, completed the route to Birmingham with its own station in Midland Road. For the first time Nuneaton had direct access to Birmingham. This fast-growing city had an almost insatiable demand for coal, brick and road stone; Nuneaton had an abundance of these resources and now the means to transport them.

The L.N.W.R. and the Midland were to come into conflict over the final local rail route. The companies compromised and formed the Ashby and Nuneaton Joint Railway of 1873, a case of seeing a gap on the railway map to be filled before any opposition could. Apart from its mineral traffic, the line served largely rural districts and never proved really profitable. The Nuneaton-Birmingham line was the obvious spur for the rapid expansion of local extractive industries, though other factors such as entrepreneurship and availability of capital are equally important. Between 1855 and 1904 nine new collieries were established deep into the coal field. The Newdegate family gave up its active interest in mining and leased all the mines and coal reserves on the Arbury estate to the Griff Colliery Company Limited in 1882. This

89   Griff Crossings in 1968. In addition to the public railways around Nuneaton, numerous private lines from local collieries fed into the main system. The line south of Bermuda village served Stanley's and Haunchwood brickyards and the Griff collieries.

90   Abbey Street railway station. The Midland Railway opened its Birmingham to Nuneaton line in 1864, followed by the joint line to Ashby-de-la-Zouch in 1873. When Birmingham to Leicester traffic was re-routed through Trent Valley, this station was closed and demolished.

91 Griff Colliery pumping station. The Caroline and Barbara shafts stood above the deepest level in the Griff Collieries. Underground water naturally fell to this point and was raised to the surface by these two beam engines.

92 Heath End Road: Griff No. 4 Colliery, 1950. Griff No. 4 opened in 1870 and worked until 1960. Heath End Road runs between the mine and the brickyards (top left). The scene is typical of the industrial landscapes which dominated the Nuneaton area up to the 1960s.

company worked three mines in Nuneaton: Griff No. 4 near Heath End Road (sunk 1870), Griff No. 5 also at Heath End (1873), and Griff Clara, sunk in 1894 near Griff.

Three more collieries were in Stockingford. One of the earliest was Haunchwood, already working in the 1850s, when it was taken over by Nowells & Sons before being bought by Sir Alfred Hickman in 1882. At the highest part of Haunchwood Road, behind the *Cherry Tree*, was the old Nuneaton Colliery, run by Reginald Stanley from 1878 to 1899 when the coal was worked out. Stanley's new Nuneaton Colliery near to Whittleford Road opened in 1900. At Bucks Hill the Stockingford Colliery Company of 1872 operated the only drift mine (worked since 1855) in the area, with its 45 degree shaft driving into the hill side.

As demand grew and the older mines became less productive, new collieries were sunk almost at the workable limits of the coal field. Ansley Hall dates from 1874 but only prospered when W.G. Phillips became manager after 1880. Sir Alfred Hickman opened the second Haunchwood Colliery, the Tunnel Pit at Galley Common, in 1891 and, finally, Arley Colliery was sunk in 1904. The half century between

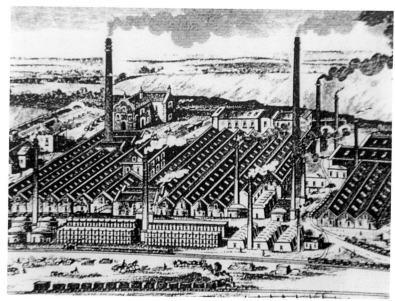

93 Haunchwood Brick & Tile Company. This sketch was on the company's letterhead in 1940 and shows the main works at the rear of Haunchwood Road. The site was cleared after closure and is now the Whittleford Country Park. The firm, founded in 1878, also had brickyards in Bermuda Road.

1860 and 1913 saw a tenfold increase in production on the coal field from 545,000 tons to over five million tons. Mining had at last become the major industrial occupation in the Nuneaton area and the largest single source of employment. The Griff Collieries alone were employing 1,101 men in 1896 and miners made up a third of the male working population in the 1911 Census.

The rapid expansion of coal mining was paralleled by growth in the brick and tile industry. Brickmaking had a continuous history through the 18th and early 19th centuries but the major impetus for growth came from two factors: railway completion and the arrival in the town of Reginald Stanley. Stanley was a Cornishman who emigrated to the United States in 1857. Having made his fortune by gold mining, he returned home ten years later and came to Nuneaton where his brother Jacob was already a partner in a Stockingford brickyard. Reginald entered the partnership in 1867 and bought out his partners in 1869 to form the company known as Stanley Brothers. Reginald Stanley became the town's greatest entrepreneur. His firm operated seven brickyards in Nuneaton, and further yards at Willenhall, Coventry and Burslem, Stoke-on-

Trent. He owned Nuneaton Colliery, leased the Charity Mine in Bedworth and founded Nuneaton Engineering Company.

The second major brickmaking concern was started by a civil engineer, James Knox. Apparently, he was passing through Stockingford by rail when his experienced eye saw a band of Etruria Marl in a cutting. To exploit this clay, he formed a partnership which became the Haunchwood Brick & Tile Company in 1878. The firm's most famous product was the very hard blue bricks made from the marl.

Coal and brick were a major factor in Nuneaton's newest industry, engineering. Again the impetus came from Reginald Stanley, who saw that future progress would be through mechanisation. Accordingly, around 1889 he set up the Nuneaton Engineering Company at the bottom of Tuttle Hill. For mining he produced two significant inventions: the heading machine, for driving through the coal, and the quartz crushing mill. Both were quicker and cheaper than manual labour, and both had good export potential. For brickmaking, Stanley invented mechanised presses which enabled one operative to produce up to 12,000 bricks or roof tiles a day. A second factor was

94 Slingsby's Silk factory, Seymour Road, 1909. Slingsby's survived the collapse of the silk trade by specialising in banners and masonic regalia. Here the workers are operating Jacquard Looms, capable of producing intricate patterns mechanically.

95 Franklin's Silk factory, Seymour Road, 1968. Franklin's of Coventry took over the long-established firm of Slingsby's. When Franklin's finally closed, some 350 years of silk working in the town came to an end.

proximity to Coventry, where cycle-making, and later motor cycles and cars, was the growing industry. Several small firms were established in Nuneaton to build bicycles including, inevitably, Birch & Co.'s George Eliot Cycles. The precision engineering skills developed from both branches of engineering were to be the foundation of the local economy in the following century.

The 1860s proved to be as significant for textiles as for extractives. The silk ribbon trade collapsed following the Cobden Treaty of 1860. *White's Directory* of 1874 lists only four master ribbon weavers in the town. The only substantial manufacturer was Henry Slingsby, whose firm survived by specialising in banners and masonic regalia. The collapse led to widespread unemployment. There are records of large-scale emigration—Bulkington parish register has a list of families who left the village—and census totals show a static population total for some thirty years. But the bulk of the weavers, especially females, tied to home and family, remained to form a pool of skilled labour, desperate for work and ready for exploitation.

Nuneaton first became an outpost of the cotton industry, logically given the well-established rail link to Lancashire. In 1860 Thomas Townsend of Coventry converted the Albion Buildings topshops to cotton spinning. A second factory was built in Attleborough Road for the Nuneaton Cotton & Weaving Company, which was taken over by Messrs Fielding & Johnson's in 1886. Two other textile concerns were the Nuneaton Wool Company of 1864 in Church Street, which later became the Union Wool and Leather Company, and Lister's of Bradford, who specialised in silk fabrics and velvet plush. Following a strike at their Manningham Mills in 1895, Samuel Lister sought an alternative source of production to meet orders and as an insurance against future unrest. Lister's first took over the Albion Buildings before erecting a new spinning mill and weaving sheds close by.

96 Fielding & Johnson's factory, Attleborough Road. The rail link to Lancashire enabled the cotton industry to expand into this area, attracted by a surplus of skilled textile workers after the collapse of the ribbon trade.

97 Lister's factory in Attleborough Road. This photograph captures the simple strong lines of the spinning mill. Lister's expanded into Nuneaton from their Bradford Manningham factory in 1895. This fine building was demolished, to be replaced by low-level industrial units.

98 Rufus Jones' factory, Attleborough Green. This simple but attractive factory building was home to yet another of the town's textile industries, elastic webbing manufacture, which developed from the declining silk trade. The site is now occupied by a Co-op superstore.

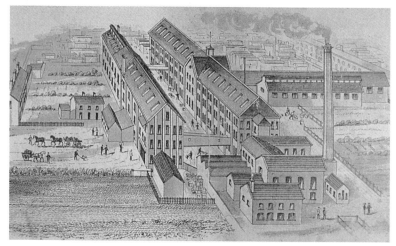

99 Hall & Phillips Hat factory, 1967. Originally built as a silk factory, this was taken over by Messrs Hall & Phillips of Atherstone in 1868, during the silk trade depression. Changing fashion ended hat making after the Second World War and the premises became industrial units. In December 1967 the buildings were severely damaged by fire and later demolished.

100   The Reliable Clothing Company, York Street. Garment making was a comparatively late entry in the town's trades but by 1900 both the Reliable and Hart and Levy's factories were well-established. Ready-made clothing production is now the only surviving textile industry.

101   Connor's Box factory, Fife Street, 1951. Connor's came originally from Coventry to these premises between Fife Street and Queen's Road. The firm acquired a second factory in Aston Road after the war.

102 Nuneaton Brewery, pre-1890. The office was in Bridge Street with the works and yard extending to Newdegate Street and Bond Gate. Brewing started in 1878 but the enterprise had little success, being up for sale in 1881, 1882 and 1890. Failure to reach the reserve price led to demolition. The Conservative Club was built on the corner site in 1899.

103 Stanley's Engineering Company. Reginald Stanley started this factory some ten years earlier to make mining, quartz-crushing and brickmaking machinery, all from the firm's patented designs. The buildings still largely survive as workshops.

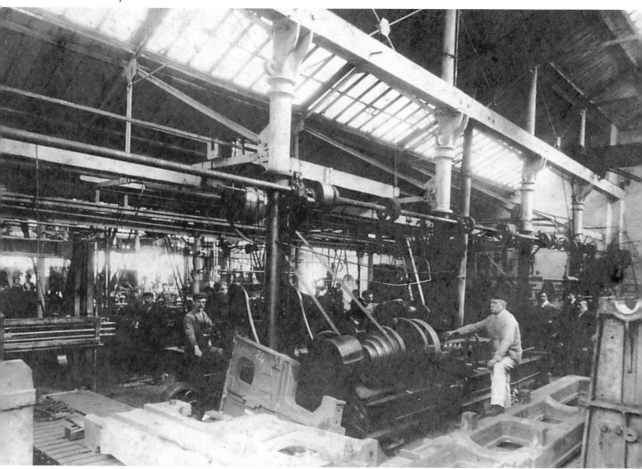

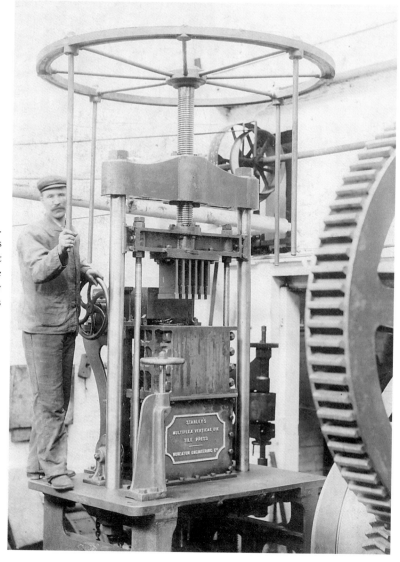

104 Stanley Patent Tile Press. Reginald Stanley and his engineers played a significant part in the mechanisation of the brick and tile industry. A Stanley press could produce 12,000 tiles in one day.

Other new industries might be termed textile-related since they used similar skills. Typical was the hat industry traditionally centred on Atherstone. An old silk factory on Abbey Green was converted to hat making, and in 1868 Hall & Phillips, seeking to expand, moved from Atherstone into an old ribbon factory in Meadow Street which they enlarged. In Attleborough, Rufus Jones built a new elastic webbing works and two clothing factories—Hart & Levy and The Reliable Clothing Company—were established in the town.

Lastly, Alfred Connor started his box-making firm with two factories in Fife Street and Aston Road.

These new textile and related trades were of great economic significance to the area. Mainly employing female labour, they provided a valuable alternative to the male-based extractive industries. The sound industrial base founded in the 1860s was to lead to increasing prosperity and rapid population growth in the four decades before the First World War.

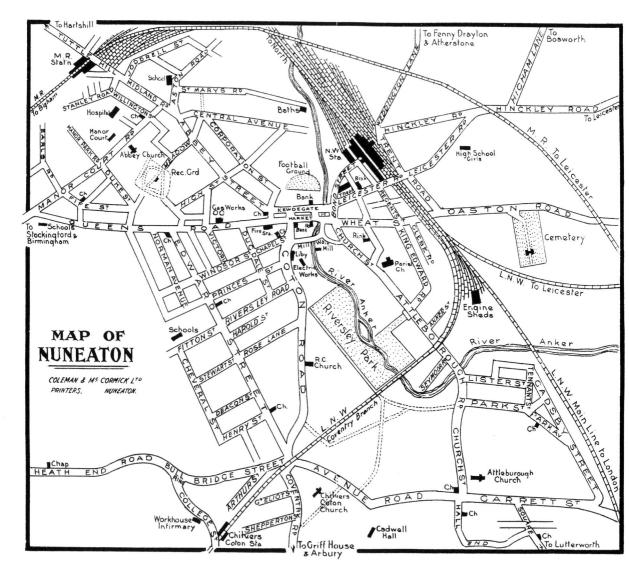

105 Nuneaton and Chilvers Coton, *c*.1910. This map marks how far the town had expanded beyond its original limits. It also shows how the railway restricted development to the east.

Eleven

URBAN GROWTH AND ITS CONSEQUENCES 1880-1914

Between 1851 and 1871 there was an absolute decline in Nuneaton's population. The figures, adjusted to cover the modern borough area, fall from 13,532 to 12,868; not a great fall but, since it was against the national trend, significant. The 1881 Census shows the first slow signs of recovery, with a rise to 13,714, but from then onwards the trend is obvious: not only is the total rising but the increase is greater each decade. The most spectacular rise occurs between 1901 and 1911, when the population leapt from 24,996 to 37,073, a 48 per cent growth in ten years, a rate never exceeded before or since.

The most obvious effect of this turn of the century population explosion was the growth of new housing areas. Even as late as 1881, Nuneaton town occupied much the same area as it did in Tudor and even medieval times. It was impossible to accommodate the rising population in the existing built-up area so new streets of terraced houses began to grow around the old town and village centres. The earliest expansion was south of Wash Lane (Queen's Road), in Dugdale and Victoria Streets, followed by Alexandra Street. The largest of the new suburbs was at the west end of the town, either side of the new Manor Court Road and north of Abbey Green. Attleborough expanded between the two main textiles factories, Lister's and Fielding & Johnson's, Coton below the Coventry Canal, and Stockingford around Church Road. The financial impetus came from

countless, now largely unknown, petty landlords who bought and built on blocks of land along the new streets. Many houses still have name and date plaques which bear mute testimony to this haphazard development.

A second form of development was the building of mining villages. Because the deep coal seams were outside the existing town area and local transport non-existent, mining companies needed to house their workers close to the new pits. The best example is Bermuda village, built in 1894 at £90 per house, equidistant between the Clara and no. 4 Collieries. Similar mining villages sprang up at Galley Common, Ansley Common and, later, New Arley.

In the 1851 Census Dr Edward Nason, the leading surgeon, lived in an imposing Abbey Street house amid the squalor of the courts. Housing was not segregated by class. Only those of, or aspiring to, gentry status had their country estates outside the urban areas: Attleborough Hall, Caldwell Hall, Camp Hill Hall and Weddington Castle. By the end of the century the rising middle classes had started to create more exclusive housing. The nearest to a middle-class suburb is the area around Reginald Stanley's Manor Court which has many substantial houses such as Lansdowne Terrace in Manor Court Road, Hospital Drive and Earls Road. But even these streets have their rows of terraced working-class houses. The most significant expansion was across the Trent

106 Queen's Road was originally called Wash Lane. The street did not develop until the Wash Brook, which ran along it, was culverted. With the council offices and fire station (left), and new shops and houses, Queen's Road became the principal street of the expanding town.

107 Charlie Wilson standing outside his house in Bermuda village. With the coal seams dipping south-west, many of the new deep mines were remote from the built-up areas. This led the colliery companies to build their own villages. Typical was Bermuda village, built in 1894 between the two Griff Colliery mines.

108 Gadsby Street and Tennant Street, Attleborough. The area between Lister's and Fielding & Johnson's textile factories became a new area of working-class housing in the late 19th century.

109 Princes Street, Nuneaton, *c.*1904. Urban expansion south of Queen's Road was mainly of working-class housing, though these Princes Street villas aspired to higher status. The centre one of the three gabled houses was occupied by nurses, the first step towards the town's hospital.

110   Manor Court Road: Lansdowne Terrace, *c*.1904. Industrial and commercial progress brought an increase in the town's middle and professional classes. Manor Court Road, then on the edge of the town, was a desirable area and became the first middle-class suburb.

Valley Railway into Old Hinckley Road, Leicester Road and just into Hinckley Road itself, foreshadowing the ribbon development of the inter-war years.

This period also saw major re-building in the town centre as commercial reflected industrial growth. The lead came from the banks, with Barclays, Midland, Westminster and Lloyds all erecting imposing buildings around the Market Place and Newdegate Square. Population growth and increased purchasing power attracted the earliest national chain stores—Lipton's, Maypole Dairies, George Mason's and Boots the Chemists—alongside the old family shops. Perhaps the most significant development came from the Co-operative Movement. The fledgeling society raised £40 capital and rented for seven shillings a week a small shop, 119 Abbey Street, which opened for business on 12 April

1884. As trade expanded so did the Co-op, buying its first property opposite the original shop after two years, while further acquisitions led to a new purpose-built store in 1903.

By 1914 Nuneaton had two hotels. The earlier was Reginald Stanley's *Gate Temperance Hotel* of 1898 on the corner of Abbey Gate, which still survives as the most strikingly impressive and individual example of local architecture. Just before the outbreak of war the old *Newdegate Arms Inn* was demolished, to be replaced by the imposing *Newdegate Arms Hotel*. Leisure, too, changed the townscape. The Edwardian period saw the replacement of many of the old public houses by more imposing buildings. The *Crown*, Bond Gate, *Queen's Head*, Church Street and the *Plough and Ball*, Abbey Green typified the new pub architecture, while on an even grander scale were the

111 *The Gate Hotel*, Abbey Gate. Prominent Methodist Reginald Stanley built this temperance hotel in 1898. A mock–Tudor fantasy, it uses many of Stanley Brothers' products. The hotel closed in 1908 and became shops and offices. Apart from the rebuilt ground floor this striking building has survived largely intact.

112 Newdegate Square and Henry Lester's house with the National Provincial Bank on its right and Lloyd's Bank on the left.

113   Bridge Street from the Market Place. This photograph shows clearly the narrow entrance into the Market Place. The *Bull Hotel* still retained its central archway, indicating a coaching past. The Post Office was soon to be replaced by the later building set back to its right.

114   Attleborough Hall. Built in 1809 by solicitor George Greenway (George Eliot's lawyer Dempster), the hall later became the home of Thomas Townsend. His daughter Patty, a talented artist, married Joseph Fielding Johnson and they moved in in 1888. The hall was demolished in 1932.

115 Weddington Castle, 1917. Built on the site of an earlier manor house, Weddington Castle was an imposing mock-medieval structure. After serving as a Red Cross hospital during the First World War, the building was demolished in 1928 and much of its grounds sold for housing.

116 Camp Hill Hall. This imposing Tudor-style mansion was built by Nuneaton banker William Craddock. Demolished in 1939, only the lodge and the magnificent avenue of trees in Camp Hill Drive remain, together with Stubb's Pool, named after a later owner of the Hall.

117   Manor Court Road, 1905. The only house visible on the left side is Reginald Stanley's Manor Court, now an old people's home. Its chateau style is said to be for his wife, Marie Octave, who was French-Canadian. The parade passing by marked the unveiling of the Boer War memorial in Bond Gate.

two political clubs: Reginald Stanley's Liberal Club of 1894 and the Conservative Club and St George's Hall of 1899.

Public entertainment had long been provided by travelling players and exhibitions, as the *Nuneaton Diary* records. Perhaps the nearest to a theatre was the music hall at the *Crystal Palace* public house in the Market Place before its removal to Gadsby Street in 1909. In 1900 Bond Gate was transformed by the new Prince of Wales (later Hippodrome) Theatre with its gilded domes flanking the statue of Euterpe. Close by on Leicester Road was Vince's Theatre, more grandly entitled the Empire Assembly Hall and Skating Rink. By 1914 live theatre had been joined by silent pictures at the Royal, Princes, Palace and Scala Cinemas.

The need for public open spaces had been recognised by the Board of Health. The Medical Officer, Dr Peacock, reported in his 1892 statement to the Board: 'The Recreation Ground [off Queen's Road], which was opened in March has taken a great number of children out of the streets ... and the provision of a

large and pure breathing space has had, and will have, a most beneficial impress upon the young and rising generation'.

In 1907 Edward Melly of the Griff Collieries Company gave the land for Riversley Park, complete with bandstand, boating on the Anker and the Museum (1913). Organised sport was centred on the Newdegate Arms sports field where both Nuneaton Town and the Rugby Football Club had their grounds.

1893 brought a major change in local government when Nuneaton, Chilvers Coton, Weddington and part of Caldecote amalgamated to form a new Urban District Council. The change was marked by the erection of Council Offices and Fire Station in the newly named Queen's Road. The rapidly increasing population soon brought a bid for borough status. This was achieved when Nuneaton received its Charter of Incorporation on 12 September 1907, and celebrated on Charter Day with an enormous procession involving just about every firm, organisation and school in the town.

Both the Urban District and later Borough Councils proved to be very energetic in innovation and reform, especially in education. One of the early decisions was to adopt the Public Libraries Act and build an imposing Free Library in 1899 close to the town centre in Coton Road. The 1902 Balfour Education Act gave local authorities control over elementary education and Nuneaton formed its first Education Committee in 1903 at a time of crisis. The church schools of the 1840s had sufficient capacity while the population total remained stagnant, but once growth took off after 1881 the shortfall became all too apparent. Temporary accommodation, such as the Primitive Methodists' Sunday School building

in Edward Street, could only provide short-term relief. The Education Committee acted swiftly. In 1905 new Council Schools opened at Grove Road, Stockingford and Queen's Road, Nuneaton. Park Avenue, Attleborough was completed in September 1908 and Fitton Street, Chilvers Coton by April 1910. Not only had the council doubled the total provision in a mere five years but the buildings, with classrooms round a spacious central hall, marked a new standard in design.

Warwickshire County Council, too, helped widen educational opportunity. The greatest need was for secondary education for girls. In 1910 this was met by the Nuneaton High School for Girls in Leicester Road. Both

118   The Chase, Higham Lane. Brickyard owner James Knox built this Jacobean-style house on what was then the outskirts of the town. The Chase had ceased to be a private residence by 1939 and served as offices for the Prudential Insurance Company, evacuated during the war, before becoming the *Chase Hotel*.

119   Charter Day, 1907. Nuneaton's most important day was Saturday 28 September 1907, when the town celebrated the grant of a royal charter incorporating the Borough of Nuneaton. Borough status came about largely through population growth, but an important factor must have been the energy displayed by the earlier Urban District Council.

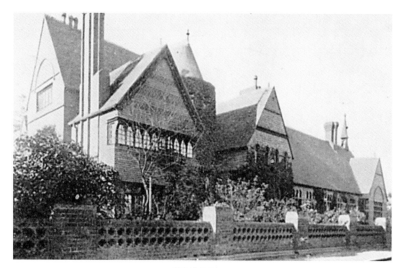

120 The new Grammar School, King Edward Road. In 1880 the school moved across the churchyard to this new building designed in the Tudor style by Clapton Rolfe, the architect of the Abbey Church nave. To the left of the school was the headmaster's house where the boarding pupils lived.

121 Nuneaton High School for Girls, Leicester Road. The opening of the High School in 1910 filled the major remaining gap in provision—secondary education for girls. Under re-organisation some sixty years later, it became comprehensive under a new name—Etone School.

122 The Hippodrome Theatre, Bond Gate. Originally called the Prince of Wales, the theatre was re-named after it opened in 1900. By the 1920s live theatre increasingly gave way to films, though the Hippodrome remained the venue for amateur productions up to its closure.

123 The Empire, Leicester Road. In Edwardian Nuneaton Vint's Theatre was a close neighbour of, and rival establishment to, the Hippodrome. Here entitled the Empire Hall and Skating Rink, the building has had a chequered history, including bus garage, car show room, bakery and now night club.

124 The Liberal Club, Abbey Street. This 1894 building also owes its foundation and architecture to Reginald Stanley, who combined nonconformity in religion with liberalism in politics. The club, built on the site of the town's first fire station, has been sympathetically restored.

125 The Council Offices, Queen's Road. The new Urban District Council of 1893 marked its status by erecting new offices with a fire station on the ground floor. When the new Council House was opened in 1934, the offices became the library. The provision of a new fire station and library in 1962 led to the building's demolition.

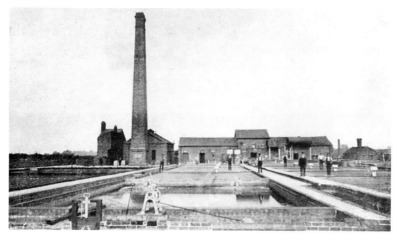

126 Sewage Works Pumping Station, 1902. The town's abiding problem had always been waste removal. The Urban District Council tackled this with characteristic energy by building a sewage treatment works at Hartshill together with this pumping station.

the High School and the boys' Grammar School, rebuilt on the King Edward Road site in 1880, were fee paying, but the county provided scholarships to enable at least some children from less affluent families to enter secondary education. This era also saw the start of post-school provision with the County Mining School of 1913 in Riversley Road, which also housed cookery and handicraft centres for use by the elementary schools.

The Public Health Board established in 1848, which had run the town up to 1893 from 'a dingy room behind the old Drill Hall near Mill Walk', had made steady if unspectacular progress, marked by a 33 per cent fall in the death rate to 18.2 per thousand between 1848 and 1892. The cesspits—the scourge of 1848—

had almost disappeared as sewers were laid through the town to the St Mary's Road pumping station. The water supply was greatly improved with reservoirs high above the town at Hartshill and Oldbury. Electricity had also come to the town when the Nuneaton Electrical Company was formed in 1897. The company was taken over by the council in 1900 and a new generating station was built between the Free Library and the river in Coton Road.

Enterprise was not confined to commercial and municipal initiative. Arguably one of the most significant advances was the campaign started by Dr Richard Nason to establish the Cottage (later Manor) Hospital. Dr Nason formed a fund-raising committee in 1890 and money was found to rent a house in Princes

127 Nuneaton General Hospital, pre-1920. The efforts of private individuals, led by Dr Richard Nason, brought about the opening of this cottage hospital in 1893. In 1920 the two wards were extended forwards to house 20 beds each, and further wards were built later, again through private generosity. The annual carnival from 1930 raised money for the hospital.

128 Riversley Park, *c.*1923. The council, already aware of the need for public open spaces in the rapidly growing town, was no doubt delighted to accept Alderman Edward Melly's gift of land for a municipal park which was opened in 1907. Named after Mr Melly's home in Liverpool, Riversley Park has been enjoyed by generations of Nuneatonians.

129   Show jumping at the Warwickshire Agricultural Society's Show, 29 August 1906, and Mr Grundy can be seen putting *Boscombe Lass* through her paces on the Newdegate Arms ground.

130   Nuneaton Rugby Football Club, 1905-6. The *Nuneaton Diary* records the formation of a Cricket Society in 1812 but organised sports clubs really date from the last quarter of that century. Nuneaton Town was the leading soccer team, and the rugby club, founded in 1879, soon had an impressive fixture list. Matches were played on the sports ground behind the *Newdegate Arms Hotel*.

Street to accommodate two nurses and limited patient care. When the appeal had exceeded £3,000 and a site been given by Reginald Stanley and James Tomkinson, plans were drawn up for the new hospital. Costing £2,794, Nuneaton Cottage Hospital, with its central administration block and two eight-bed wards, was opened on 20 September 1893. This small hospital was not suitable for infectious illnesses so the town's Medical Officer, faced with a smallpox outbreak, opened a temporary isolation hospital on Tuttle Hill which, in turn, was replaced by a new building at Bramcote in 1906.

By 1914 Nuneaton had been transformed. Imposing new buildings dominated its town centre, the worst environmental excesses (apart from slum clearance) were being tackled, and new facilities provided. More significant was the change in attitude. The Health Report of 1848 was almost fatalistic, describing everything but proposing little. In 1892 the Board's surveyor confidently stated: 'Indeed, no town of any note can be said to flourish under the old midden system. There is something repulsive in its very principle.' As the 20th century dawned, nothing seemed unachievable.

Twelve

THE 20TH CENTURY

The period following the First World War can best be described as a time of consolidation. There are no dramatic changes to match those of the pre-war decades. Nevertheless 1919-39 did see modest but still significant developments in industry and social change. Population grew steadily from 42,104 in the 1921 census to 46,521 in 1931 and an estimated 50,000 by 1941. Much of this increase can be ascribed to natural growth as the youth-biased population of the pre-war decades became the established families between the wars. A new factor was long-distance migration. The relative stability of the Warwickshire coal field during the slump attracted miners from worse-hit areas. For example, 510 families came from South Wales in 1936 and a further 214 from County Durham.

The end of the short post-war economic boom in 1921 and the ensuing slump of the mid-twenties reduced the national demand for coal. Locally the situation was met in two ways. Firstly the least productive mines, those on or near the exposed coal measures, were abandoned: Nuneaton Colliery in 1922, Haunchwood Nowell's in 1925 and Stockingford 'Dry Bread' in 1928. Then the Warwickshire Coal Owners Association agreed a quota system to cut production and share the available market. The mining labour force fell by 14.5 per cent from 5,518 in 1921 to 4,898 (1931) to 4,716 in 1939. In the same period

Warwickshire coal field production rose from 4.1 to 5.8 million tons. This higher productivity was achieved by increasing mechanisation and concentration of output on the newer, deeper collieries on the concealed coal field.

With the decline of its watch-making industry, Coventry had developed precision engineering and the assembly of bicycles and, later, motor cycles and cars. Nuneaton, as usual, came under the influence of the city. Apart from a few cycle firms in the Edwardian period, the town's role became contributory, with small, specialist component firms supplying the Coventry factories. The only major engineering factory to come to the town, significantly from Coventry, was Sterling Metals in 1939. On its greenfield Gypsy Lane site, 1,500 workers were employed in casting and machining the new ultra-lightweight metal, magnesium. But Coventry's influence was most apparent as a direct employer. According to the 1931 Census, 1,200 workers travelled daily by train or bus to the city factories.

Only one major new textile concern appeared in this period. In 1921 Courtaulds, yet another expansion from Coventry, erected a new factory which employed 1,050 workers. Its four-storeyed mill and clock tower dominated the town centre area for over seventy years. Otherwise, textiles followed the pre-war pattern of wool, cotton and silk processing and hat and hosiery manufacture. Again, these textile-based firms employed mainly females

131 Courtaulds factory, 1922. When Courtaulds, the pioneers in artificial silk, needed to expand from their Coventry factories, they came to Nuneaton with its long textile heritage and convenient canal-side site. When the factory closed, no viable use for this impressive building was found and demolition began in 1995. Only the clock has been preserved.

132   The town centre, 1926. Abbey Street along the top and Queen's Road form two sides of a triangle surrounding the medieval 20-acre Countess Close. This is an excellent example of how the early town plan survived centuries of change. The gasworks dominating the town centre dates from 1836. To the east the Co-op was expanding its stores towards Queen's Road.

133   John Cook, Town Crier, 1762-1844.

134   'Jacko' Bosworth, Town Crier in the 1930s.

while a further 800 worked in the Hinckley hosiery factories. Employment opportunities for women played a major part in achieving moderate prosperity during the depression years and were a factor in attracting migration to the town.

Greater demand for local government services meant that the existing Queen's Road council offices were increasingly inadequate. The old Town Hall in the Market Place had been sold in 1900 for £13,125, which formed the nucleus of a town hall fund, and a Coton Road site was purchased by 1910. With the possibility of aid from the Unemployment Grants Committee in 1930, the council decided to go ahead with the new building. Started in December 1931, the Council House (now the Town Hall) took two years to complete. A restrained neo-classical building using mainly local materials, it housed all the council departments together with an impressive Council Chamber, committee rooms and Mayor's Parlour. The Council House was officially opened by Sir Francis Newdegate on 26 April 1934.

The post-1880 trend, which saw new housing expand beyond the ancient town and village centres, gathered momentum between the wars when the residential area doubled in size. This expansion had a double impetus from

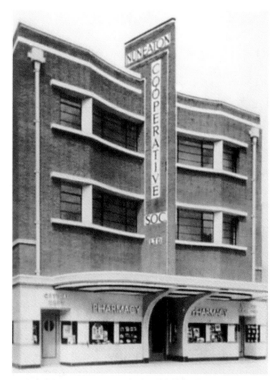

135 The Co-operative Society Pharmacy, Queen's Road, 1930s. Nuneaton has some good, if modest, examples of inter-war architecture. The pharmacy was designed in-house and shows well the new style with its curving brickwork and strong horizontal emphasis. The Co-op Hall and the Ritz Cinema were other good examples of Art Deco building.

136 Coventry Street, 1938. It seems rather strange that the first major building to be erected after the First World War was the 1919 Billiard Hall, and even stranger that it should be named after George Eliot! The building later became a hosiery factory.

137   The Council House, Coton Road. The Borough's new Council House (now re-named the Town Hall) was built between 1931 and 1933. This impressive municipal building was officially opened in 1934.

138   Coventry Road: the Wharf Bridge, pre-1926. A driver-less Midland Red bus is posed on the narrow humpback bridge over the Coventry Canal. The inter-war years saw the Birmingham-based Midland Red Company gain a near monopoly, apart from Attleborough, in the town. The bridge was replaced and widened in 1926.

139   The Regal Cinema, Lister Street, 1932. The inter-war years marked the heyday of the cinema, with five in the town centre, two more in Stockingford and Chapel End and the Regal in Attleborough. This photo was taken during the 1932 flood. The Regal was badly damaged in the 1941 air raid and pulled down.

140   The swimming baths in St Mary's Road. Nuneaton's only swimming facility was this open-air pool, converted from a settlement tank. Next to the sewage pumping station and the refuse destructor, it was a far from ideal site, though the patrons seemed to enjoy it.

government acts which subsidised council house building and the new demand for mainly low-cost private houses for sale. The Borough Council started its programme of building houses in the mid-1920s. The earliest estates were close to the centres of Stockingford and Attleborough and the Hill Top Estate off College Street. The major development of the 1930s was in the Blackatree Road/Circle area, where there was an abundance of low value old industrial land fairly close to the working collieries to the west of the town. In all 1,519

council houses were built before government subsidies were withdrawn and further construction brought to an end.

The major problem facing the council was the urgent need for slum clearance. The Medical Officer for Health reported in 1919 that in Abbey Street alone there were 136 properties which had only one living room, one bedroom, no piped water and shared earth closets. Lack of finance delayed demolition until 1935, when one Abbey Street court of four houses was cleared, followed by sub-standard dwellings in Gladstone Square (behind Bond Gate) and Back Street in 1937. By 1939 some 536 houses had been demolished.

Up to 1914 private housing for sale was largely limited to the small middle-class and professional market, while the working classes tended to rent accommodation from numerous petty landlords who had developed the terraced streets around the town centre. Relative prosperity, the availability of cheap land as farming declined and less stringent mortgages from the expanding building societies created a new market for private housing. The initial impetus came from a government grant of £75 per dwelling for private subsidised houses. This led to 591 homes being built, mainly between 1925 and 1928, before the grants ended. In all 2,892 private houses were built in the inter-war years, some 60 per cent of the increased housing stock. The main area for growth was Weddington, where land first became available following the demolition of the Castle in 1928, and large private estates were developed both east and

west of Weddington Lane. At an average price of £350, these properties found a ready market among working-class families with relatively secure occupations. In a similar fashion, Highfield Road and the neighbouring streets were carved out of the grounds of Attleborough Hall (demolished in 1932), and new housing off Camp Hill Road started with the demise of Camp Hill Hall in 1934.

For the sufficiently affluent, ribbon development along most of the main roads out of the town was the more attractive option. Aided by increasingly affordable private cars and regular Midland Red bus services, ribbon development married the convenience of easy transport to the attraction of a semi-rural location. Hinckley Road and the Long Shoot, Higham Lane and Lutterworth Road became the new largely middle-class areas. Desirable though many of these large, individually-designed houses were, ribbon development created the illusion that Nuneaton was built up almost to the borough boundaries, hiding areas

141 Hill Top Estate: Marner Road, 1984. Council housing started in the mid-1920s with the aim of providing cheap rented accommodation and aiding slum clearance. These council houses of the 1930s were well-built, quite spacious and of a pleasantly varied design—a great advance in working-class dwellings.

142 The Emergency Hospital, College Street. Completed in 1940 to cater for potential military casualties, this served as a military hospital for the duration of the war. It then became the nucleus of the George Eliot Hospital. The single-storey wards are still in use though the corridors, here open to the elements, are now enclosed.

of countryside almost from view. Similar growth to the south and north of the town created a sprawling urban corridor most of the way from Coventry to Hinckley.

Arguably the most impressive development was in education. The raising of the school-leaving age to 14 in 1918 could be met by establishing senior departments in all-age schools, or by building new senior council schools. The forward-looking Borough Education Committee chose the second option where finance allowed. The earliest of the new senior schools was Manor Park, which opened in 1928, followed by Swinnerton School in 1932. Two further schools, Arbury and Higham Lane, both opened in 1939.

The earlier two of these schools provided new standards of accommodation far removed from the council schools of a mere twenty years before. Set in spacious grounds with playing fields, they had veranda-style classrooms with glass walls on two sides and cookery and wood-work centres. Arbury and Higham Lane were even more advanced, having specialist rooms for arts and sciences. Ratepayers were known to complain about profligacy but the far-sighted Education Committee had advanced the scope of elementary education to what would only be achieved nationally after 1944.

The Second World War

For many parts of Britain the Second World War brought the experience of death and destruction at first hand for the first time. Nuneaton was no exception; its close proximity to arms and munitions factories in Coventry made the town an inevitable target.

The earliest air raid, though, came almost by accident. A lone German bomber jettisoned its load over built-up Weddington, destroying six houses, seriously damaging 50 more and causing the first civilian casualties: three dead and six injured. Nuneaton escaped the great Coventry blitz of November 1940, only to become the German target on the night of 17 May 1941. Most parts of the town suffered damage but worst hit were the Chilvers Coton/Heath End area and east of the town centre. Coton lost two churches. Only the tower and chancel of All Saints withstood both high explosive and incendiary bombs while Edward Street Methodists was completely destroyed. The houses on the west side of Church Street, with their George Eliot connections, were largely reduced to rubble, and The Elms in Vicarage Street, the author's first school, was badly damaged. A hundred people died that night, including Edward Melly, benefactor and former mayor, and his wife. The last major

143 Church Street air raid aftermath, 1941. The night of 17 May 1941 brought Nuneaton's heaviest air raid. Many Church Street premises were severely damaged, including Alderman Melly's house, The Croft (far left), and the houses which appeared in George Eliot's *Scenes of Clerical Life*.

144 Vicarage Street, 1941. Both Vicarage Street School and The Elms, where George Eliot was educated, were severely damaged in the May air raid, though nearby St Nicolas Church fortunately survived almost intact. The destruction of many of the west side buildings, including the Tribune printing works, cleared the way for redevelopment and the new ring road.

145   Chilvers Coton: All Saints Church, 1941. From a historical point of view, the worst loss inflicted by bombing was arguably the destruction of Coton church with its close George Eliot associations. Under the inspired leadership of the Rev. R.T. Murray, German prisoners-of-war rebuilt the church which was re-consecrated in September 1947.

146   Coton Road: royal visit, 1942. To mark Nuneaton's sufferings in the blitz, the town was honoured to receive a visit from King George VI and Queen Elizabeth. Here they are being introduced to Civil Defence workers outside the Council House on 25 February 1942.

raid came on 25 June 1942, when the Manor Court area suffered most and a further 18 persons were killed.

The war brought a second hospital to Nuneaton under the Emergency Medical Service in 1940. Long known locally simply as 'The Emergency', this six-ward, 200-bed hospital was built at the rear of the Work-house. Planned to take military casualties, the hospital was also pressed into use after the Coventry blitz, Nuneaton's main air raid and, paradoxically, to treat Germans from local prisoner-of-war camps.

In all, 131 civilians died and 229 were injured. The estimated 291 high explosive and thousands of incendiary bombs which fell on the town destroyed 380 houses and over ten thousand more needed repairs. The air raids were met with heroism—Dr P.G. Horsburgh G.M., James Shannon B.E.M. and Mary Maybury M.B.E. were among those decorated—and humour: one trader whose

plate-glass window was blown in proudly announced 'open now more than ever'. One unique gesture of reconciliation was the re-building of Coton Church by German prisoners-of-war from the camp on the Arbury Hall estate.

Modern Town

The post-war period saw the population grow steadily from 54,407 in 1951 to 66,979 twenty years later. The late 1940s 'baby boom' undoubtedly explained part of this increase but immigration continued to be the major factor as Nuneaton shared Coventry's industrial success. One completely new aspect of the pattern was immigration from overseas. The earliest wave came mainly from Eastern Europe, from where men were recruited by the National Coal Board and housed initially on hostels off Camp Hill Road. The brick and tile companies also recruited workers from Italy. The 1960s brought the first migrants from the Indian

147   Marston Lane: Sterling Metals Ltd, c.1954. Sterling Metals were attracted to Nuneaton in 1939 by the offer of a greenfield site with all services provided by the council. Vital for the war effort with its production of magnesium alloys, the company declined in the changing post-war world and eventually closed this factory. The whole area is now given over to housing.

sub-continent, attracted to the town by textile work, followed by Indians forced out of Kenya. Though never numerically large, the Asian communities have brought new and distinctive cultures to the town.

The employment pattern continued the pre-war trends. By 1951 engineering trades had become the largest group with 4,324 workers. The extractive industries lost their pre-eminence, falling to 3,398, while textiles and allied trades employed 3,127 workers, including 2,376 women. More people than ever—9,153 in total—were making the daily journey out of town to work: more than 5,000 to Coventry and Bedworth, 1,500 to Hinckley. Nuneaton was increasingly becoming a dormitory town.

The local rise to supremacy of the engineering trades still had its roots in Coventry. The new small industrial estates located near centres of population in Weddington, Caldwell, Camp Hill and, later, Whitacre Road and Bermuda were ideal for small specialist concerns supplying components to the Coventry motor and machine tool trades. The one large new factory was Clarkson's, who transferred to Nuneaton the day after the destruction of their Coventry premises in November 1940.

The coal industry was sustained in the early post-war years by the national shortage of fuel, and the coal field was still producing 1.7 million tons as late as 1957. As oil became increasingly available and correspondingly cheaper, so the demand for coal fell and every colliery within the borough closed within two decades. First to go were the three oldest mines: Griff Clara in 1955, Ansley Hall after working 81 years in 1959, and Griff No. 4 the following year. The last remaining 19th-century pit, Haunchwood, closed in 1967, and Arley a year later. When Newdigate Colliery at Bedworth closed in 1982 the last remaining mine on the coalfield was the ultra-modern, very deep Daw Mill, beyond the Arley Fault, which only opened in 1958. With colliery buildings demolished and spoil banks carted away or land-scaped, little remains now to mark what had once been the area's greatest industry.

Textiles and related trades experienced some twenty years of stability and even growth. One new sector was boot and shoe manufacture, typified by Finn's and D. & R. Closers, who came to the town after facing labour shortages in Northamptonshire. The period also saw the end of over three centuries of silk weaving with the closure of Franklin's, the Coventry firm which had taken over the long-established Slingsby's Ribbon factory. Textile production fell as cheap imports captured the market. One by one the tall factories which, with the collieries and brickyards, had dominated the landscape faced demolition. Even the new shoe factories did not see out the end of the century.

The eventual decline in extractive and manufacturing industries was not matched by urban decline. Air-raid destruction, unfit dwellings and a six-year ban on house building had created a large shortage. The immediate need was for low-cost housing, and government restrictions on private building led to a huge expansion of council estates. The largest development was at Camp Hill where 1,400 houses were built by 1956. Almost as extensive were the three estates on the eastern side of the borough at Hill Top, Caldwell and Marston Lane, with 1,131 houses by 1958. New to municipal housing were blocks of flats built mainly on central bomb and slum clearance sites.

Up to 1958 only 400 private dwellings had been built for sale. From then onwards few council houses were erected while private estates burgeoned in Weddington, St Nicolas, White Stone and off Ansley Road in Stockingford. With the exception of Glendale, largely built on old industrial sites, the new estates occupied former farmland. With the completion of the latter Horeston Grange and Galley Common, Nuneaton had built up almost to its boundaries, with the only pockets of agricultural land left at its peripheries.

148 Ironmonger's shop, Queen's Road. Horace Collett and his wife are standing outside their shop, whose interior was as packed as the pavement outside. Collett's was typical of the small family businesses which have been gradually edged out by chain stores and, later, supermarkets. Happily some truly local firms still survive to give the town its individuality.

Town centre redevelopment proved to be a mixture of enlightened planning and often deplorable fulfilment. The council commissioned distinguished architect Frederick Gibberd to produce a plan for a new administrative centre to the east of Church Street. This brought together all the Crown Offices, Police Station and Magistrates' Court, Post Office and Library and, unwittingly, returned the town's centre to its Anglo-Saxon site. With the notable exception of Gibberd's own design for the Library, the architecture was undistinguished.

The same applied to commercial rebuilding, especially in Bridge Street and the Market Place, where the 1960s—a generally depressing time for architecture—saw the replacement of many fine individual buildings with standard retail units. The new doctrine of conservation areas came too late to save buildings like the *Newdegate Arms Hotel*, but planners are now more aware of what remains of the town centre heritage.

Nuneaton's greatest problem is traffic. Two major trunk roads, the A47 and A444,

149 Coton Road police station and magistrates' court. The earliest recorded police station was in Abbey Street while the magistrates met in the old *Newdegate Arms Hotel*. Both services were brought together by the County Council in this imposing new building which also contained the office of the first County Mining School Principal (far left).

150 *The Newdegate Arms Hotel* was built on the site of the old hotel in 1914. It, too, has subsequently been demolished.

151 Church Street, 1968. Nuneaton's master-planner, Frederick Gibberd, designed the new Library which opened in 1962. Its simple façade does not clash with the highly decorated line of the church and the two buildings stand well together. Placing all the new administrative buildings east of the river brought the town back to its Anglo-Saxon origins.

intersect in the town centre, while the spread of housing estates has generated much local traffic. Successive town and county councils have failed to find an adequate solution. The earliest idea, the opening up of the town centre by widening Bridge Street, only added to congestion. The dualling of Coton Road to link with the extended Bedworth by-pass, the construction of Roanne and Vicarage Street Ringways, and pedestrianisation of the town centre have only proved a partial success. The latest scheme, the construction of an eastern relief road, has helped divert traffic from the centre, but only at the expense of cutting Attleborough in half.

Educational provision continued to be Nuneaton's finest achievement. Its pre-war successes led to the granting of Excepted District status under the 1944 Act and the Education Department coped well with changing demand. The senior schools of the inter-war years became secondary moderns and, with the building of the Alderman Smith, St Joseph's and George Eliot Schools, provided a good standard of facilities across the borough. King Edward VI Grammar and the Girls High Schools both became non-feepaying and with Manor Park, which became a Technical Grammar School in 1956, provided education up to university entrance.

Primary provision was improved after 1954 by building new schools to replace old accommodation and to serve all the new housing areas. The erection of a workshop block on the Hinckley Road site in 1961 marked the first stage of a County Further Education College for the North Warwickshire area. Within two decades provision had been

152   Vicarage Street Church of England School on its last day before the school closed down, on 17 July 1970.

transformed to cover the whole spectrum from special needs to adult education—no mean achievement for a small local authority within the wider county area.

The passing of the 1948 National Assistance Act brought the end of the workhouse though the College for the Poor did survive for a few more years as Coton Lodge, an ill-chosen old people's home. As purpose-built homes and sheltered accommodation were built, so the unfortunate Lodge finally closed and the site was made available for expansion as 'The Emergency' became the George Eliot Hospital. With the closing of the Manor Hospital in 1993, all the main services came together on the one site with purpose-built accommodation, though the informed eye can still make out the workhouse infirmary and 'The Emergency' wards.

The end of Nuneaton's history as a single entity came in 1974 when local government reorganisation brought a merger with its neighbour to form the Borough of Nuneaton and Bedworth two years later. With a 1981 population of 113,521, it became the largest urban area in a now truncated Warwickshire. The new borough found itself at the centre of the national motorway system and, as manufacturing industries began to decline, transport and warehousing firms moved in to exploit the town's location. From agriculture to industry to distribution, the history of the town has been shaped by the willingness of the locals to adapt to ever-changing circumstances. When Nuneaton gained its borough charter, it chose the motto 'prêt d'accomplir'. The town's survival over the centuries has indeed depended on its willingness to be ready to accomplish.

Sources and Further Reading

Manuscript Material

Where appropriate, primary source references are cited in the text.

The major collection of pre-1700 Nuneaton documents is the British Library Aston Papers. Particular use has been made of: Additional Roll 49466 for peasant obligations, Additional Charters 48673, 48686-7 for the Horeston Fields dispute, Additional Manuscript 36909 ff. 1-59 for the 1543/4 Constable Rental, Lichfield Joint Record Office for Nuneaton wills and probate inventories, Warwick County Record Office DR 61, 1-4 for Nuneaton parish registers, 1588-1754, Public Record Office for Enumerators' Returns for the 1851 Census.

Printed Primary Material

John Astley, *Memorandum Book of Occurrences at Nuneaton 1810-1845* [sc. the *Nuneaton Diary*] (Nuneaton Library)

G.T. Clarke, *Report on the Health and Sanitary Condition of the Inhabitants of Nuneaton and Chilvers Coton*, 1849

J. Fletcher, *Reports from Assistant Handloom Weavers Commissioners*, vol. 24, 1840

J. Morris (ed.), *Domesday Book: Warwickshire* (1976)

Lay Subsidy Roll for Warwickshire, 1332. Dugdale Society

The Registers of John of Gaunt. Camden Society, Third Series vol.20

P. Thorpe, *Printed Maps of Warwickshire* (1959 for Henry Beighton)

Warwickshire County Council Hearth Tax Rolls, vol. I, 1957

Warwickshire County Council Quarter Sessions Records, 1625-96, vols. 1-9 (1939-1964)

Secondary Sources and Further Reading

J. Burton and J. Bland, *Nuneaton Hospitals. The First Hundred Years* (1994)

D. Gover, etc., *The Place Names of Warwickshire* (1936)

K. Hughes, *George Eliot. The Last Victorian* (1998)

A.V. Jenkinson, *Some Account of St Mary's Priory Nuneaton* (1922)

D. Milburn, *Nuneaton the Growth of a Town* (Nuneaton Library 1962)

G. Nares, *Arbury Hall* (1969)

E.N. Nason, *History of Nuneaton Grammar School* (1936)

Nuneaton Observer, *Nuneaton Past and Present* (1901)

D. Patterson and I. Rowney, *St Nicolas Church Nuneaton* (1985)

E.A. Veasey, *Nuneaton in the Making* vols 1-3 (1984)

E.A. Veasey, *From Eaton to Nuneaton: A History of St Mary's Abbey* (2000)

Victoria County History Warwickshire vol. 2 (1908)

Victoria County History Warwickshire vol. 4 (1947)

S.E. West, *Griff Manor House* (Sudeley Castle) (1968)

Index